AN AMERICAN JOURNEY

AN AMERICAN JOURNEY

JOURNEY

The Presidential Campaign
Speeches of
GEORGE McGOVERN

RANDOM HOUSE NEW YORK

All rights reserved under International and Pan-American Copyright
Conventions. Published in the United States by Random House, Inc.,
New York, and simultaneously in Canada by Random House of Canada
Limited, Toronto.

Library of Congress Cataloging in Publication Data

McGovern, George Stanley, 1922–
  An American Journey.

  1. United States—Politics and government—1969–
—Addresses, essays, lectures. 2. Presidents—United
States—Election—1972. 3. McGovern, George Stanley,
1922–   I. Title.
E840.8.M34A52   329.3′01   73–20595
ISBN 0–394–48944–2 (hardbound)
ISBN 0–394–70980–2 (paperbound)

Manufactured in the United States of America
9876543
First Edition

Photographs by Stanley Tretick

To my wife Eleanor and all the McGovern volunteers

Contents

DESTINATIONS

DIRECTIONS

LOOKING AHEAD

Preface by George McGovern

The journey began during the first days of 1971 with an announcement of candidacy in my home state of South Dakota; it ended there almost two years later with a concession, a few tears, and a flood of memories. In between, there were costly tactical errors and head-filling triumphs, moments of discouragement and elation, an unpredicted springtime of victories and the final predicted defeat in the fall. I saw and was seen by literally millions of Americans. I spoke to tens of thousands personally, and they spoke with me. I went from the white mountains of New Hampshire to the Central Valley of California. I experienced the America of snow and sunshine, factories and farms, cities and countryside. I talked with some farmers who were planting, and with others who were harvesting; to crowds in shirtsleeves, and in overcoats; from one ocean to another, in every corner of the continent, through eight seasons of time and two hundred thousand miles of space.

In the end, the voters rejected me and embraced Richard Nixon—not narrowly, but decisively. Yet on that November night in Sioux Falls when the news came—news that was not unexpected, but now at last unchangeable—the disappointment was tempered by a deeper satisfaction. For I had been privileged as few others before me to know America, to touch the hands of so many who share my country, to hear their views and to reach them with my voice. Whether it was a single face at a rally, or the shape of the land as it looked from a plane thirty thousand feet in the air, what I saw day after day, month after month, was the diversity of America.

This book is a partial record of my words on that journey, of what I thought and how I reacted during the longest and widest-ranging political campaign in our history. The words are rooted in the values I learned as a young man in South Dakota; they are addressed to the problems I believe the nation must resolve in the 1970's; and they reflect the feelings of many people, gathered in a thousand different encounters, large and small, as I sought to listen as well as to speak.

Millions of Americans voted for me because of what I said; millions more voted the other way. I perceived my speeches as a way to draw the issues and win support, and in that sense they obviously were not a complete success. But to me they were a way to fulfill an obligation as well as a purpose. After years of disillusion, with more and more Americans tending to distrust and disbelieve their leadership, I was convinced that it was the obligation of every candidate to conduct an open and straightforward effort, to state his specific plans and not just his general goals, and to permit his mistakes, too, to come within public view, because that is the price of candor and an open campaign.

Many of my speeches set forth detailed proposals on hard issues. Some critics said that made bad politics. They may have been right, but I do not regret it, and I think the people will come increasingly to demand it. The speeches also reveal that sometimes I modified my views. It would have been difficult to avoid that, given my commitment to take specific stands. But I would not have had it otherwise, and I think that future voters will prefer knowing when a candidate changes his mind to not knowing what he has in mind. And I also believe my public philosophy has been marked by a reasonable consistency that will stand the scrutiny of time.

Most of all, these speeches are my imperfect attempt to express the hopes and beliefs of millions who joined in the journey

I made. We did not prevail in 1972; but I believe our failure was in the deficiencies of the campaign and the public's impression of it, not in the worth of our ideas or the ideals of the American people. And the forces of grass-roots politics did make important progress. The young who slept on floors in the primaries, the volunteers of every age who canvassed door to door, the citizens of every race who contributed ten or twenty-five dollars so a campaign for the people could be financed by the people—they can count great gains as well as a record loss. They opened the doors of the Democratic Party wider than ever before—and those doors will not soon be closed again. They speeded a different course for America in Asia. They discouraged some of the worst plans of special-interest government, such as a national sales tax. They worked hard; they gave their hearts; they were a happy band in search of, not a better break for themselves, but a better land for every citizen. That is a purpose I shall continue to seek with them.

These speeches may not be long remembered; what a defeated candidate says seldom is. But I can never forget the work of those who stood together in 1972 to bring America home to its enduring ideals. I believe they will ultimately finish this journey in victory for the land we love. It is to them and to my devoted family—Eleanor, my daughters and my son—that these words are dedicated again, as they were when they were first spoken during the campaign.

George McGovern
Washington, D.C.
November, 1973

MILESTONES

The Announcement:
A Journey Begins

On January 18, 1971, I launched the longest formally announced presidential campaign in American history.

Traditionally, the way to find out who is running for the presidency has been to ask which prospective candidates are vehement in denying even the slightest interest in that office. So it was that many commentators listed non-announced candidates as the serious possibilities. And few believed that I should be taken seriously after I said so early that I was seeking the presidency. I was undertaking an effort seen as hopeless from the start by the country's most respected political analysts, most of whom thought I would be counted out before the primaries even began.

The chances were indeed doubtful. But I was convinced that the American people yearned for a new kind of politics, based first of all upon a commitment to candor, and then upon the renewal of the nation's founding ideals. I felt that the early announcement would itself be seen as a refreshing change from the standard disclaimers. I also felt it would help me reach a wider national audience through the media and the press, so I could compete more effectively with candidates who were better known. So, with the election nearly two years away, I declared my candidacy, first in a televised address in Sioux Falls, South Dakota, and the next day at a press conference back in Washington.

Today I announce my candidacy for the presidency of the United States. My wife Eleanor and I have come home to South Dakota to make this announcement because here we shaped our basic political faith; here we were given the opportunity of public service. We are grateful for that opportunity and for your faith. We shall conduct this new effort to the honor of South Dakota, the nation, and ourselves.

My fellow South Dakotans have not always agreed with my position on public issues. That was especially true in the early 1960's when I stood almost alone in opposition to the sending of American troops to Southeast Asia. Despite these differences, you have rewarded my willingness to state my convictions freely and honestly. I anticipate the same fair hearing from citizens across the land. Thoughtful Americans understand that the highest patriotism is not to blindly accept official policy, but to love one's country deeply enough to call her to a higher standard.

I seek the presidency because I believe deeply in the American promise, and I can no longer accept the diminishing of that promise. Our country began with a declaration of man's right to "life, liberty and the pursuit of happiness." These liberating ideas gave such meaning and purpose to the new American nation that our forebears proclaimed: "We mutually pledge to each other our Lives, our Fortunes, and Our Sacred Honor."

But today, our citizens no longer feel that they can shape their own lives in concert with their fellow citizens. Beyond that is the loss of confidence in the truthfulness and common sense of our leaders. The most painful new phrase in the American political vocabulary is "credibility gap"—the gap between rhetoric and reality. Put bluntly, it means that people no longer believe what their leaders tell them.

In this decade, when we are about to observe the two-hundredth anniversary of our country, we have a new opportunity to square the nation's practices with its founding ideals. As we enter this period, we must undertake a reexamination of our ideals, institutions, and the actual conditions of our life that is just as fundamental as the discussions of the Founding Fathers two centuries ago.

A public figure today can perform no greater service than to lay bare the proven malfunctions of our society, try honestly to confront our problems in all their complexity, and stimulate the search for solutions. This is my intention in this campaign. And through my candidacy I intend to offer the American people a choice—not between parties or ideologies, not between liberal and conservative or right and left. The choice is whether our civilization can serve the freedom and happiness of every citizen, or whether we will become the ever more helpless servants of a society we have raised up to rule our lives.

This issue is, of course, a cloak for many problems. Almost everyone senses the danger and almost no one can grasp its full dimensions or honestly claim to be possessed of full and sufficient answers. One thing, however, is very clear. We will not be helped to understanding by leadership built on image-making or television commercials; by those who seek power by backroom deals, coalitions of self-interest, or a continual effort to adjust their policies and beliefs to every seeming shift in public sentiment.

The kind of campaign I intend to run will rest on candor and reason; it will be rooted not in the manipulation of our fears and divisions, but in a national dialogue based on mutual respect and common hope. That kind of campaign takes time. And that is why I am making this announcement far ahead of the traditional date. People can be frightened, amazed, and impressed in a moment. Reason and the communication of humane sentiment take longer. They are, however, more lasting and more powerful. And I have no doubt that the American people will think long and soberly before making the crucial decision of 1972.

For my part, I make one pledge above all others—to seek and speak the truth with all the resources of mind and spirit I command.

There is no higher standard to which our nation can repair

than to the ideals in our founding documents. So, as a candidate for the presidency, I shall seek to call America home to those principles that gave us birth. I have found no better blueprint for healing our troubled land than is contained in the Declaration of Independence, the Constitution, and the Bill of Rights. And I find a nation drifting so far from those ideals as to almost lose its way.

But while our problems are great, certain steps can be taken to recover the confidence of the nation. The greatness of our nation is not confined to the past, but beckons us to the future.

What are the steps to future greatness?

First, we must have the courage to admit that however sincere our motives, we made a dreadful mistake in trying to settle the affairs of the Vietnamese people with American troops and bombers. I have opposed that intervention from the beginning, while our President and other presidential prospects were supporting it. There is now no way to end it and to free our prisoners except to announce a definite, early date for the withdrawal of every American soldier. I make that pledge without reservation.

The tragedy of Vietnam does not mean that we are without vital interests abroad. Ironically, our obsession with Saigon has led to the neglect of such truly essential interests as the good will of Latin America; the survival of Israel and peace in the Middle East; and the opening of relations with China, where one third of the human race resides.

We are not likely to meet our responsibilities either at home or abroad until we remove the Southeast Asia albatross from our necks. That is the first order of business.

At home, we are beset by a most serious economic recession. This is the clearest weakness of the present Administration—a weakness marked by the worst inflation and the most severe unemployment in a decade. But that economic crisis can be solved by a coherent effort to gear our resources to the real needs of our society.

Ending the drain of Southeast Asia would relieve part of the inflationary pressure. Basing our defense budget on actual needs rather than imaginary fears would lead to further savings. Needless war and military waste contribute to the economic crisis not only through inflation, but by the dissipation of labor and resources in nonproductive enterprise.

For too long the taxes of our citizens and revenues desperately needed by our cities and states have been drawn into Washington and wasted on senseless war and unnecessary military gadgets. Each month, Washington wastes enough on military folly to rebuild an American city or give new life to a rural area. A major task of the 1970's is the conversion of our economy from the excesses of war to the works of peace. I urgently call for conversion planning to use the talent and resources that are surplus to our military-space requirements for modernizing our industrial plant and meeting other peacetime needs.

There would be work for all if we set about the job of rebuilding our cities, renewing our rural economy, reconstructing our transportation system, and reversing the dangerous pollution of our air, lakes, and streams.

A program of tax and credit incentives, combined with family farm income supports, would not only revitalize rural America but would reverse the flow of people into already congested cities.

These tasks call for an expanding economy, an adequate money supply, reasonable interest rates, and the selective use of wage and price guidelines.

Beyond these essential economic questions, we must reshape our institutions, our technology, our bureaucracy, and our political process so that they become our servants, not our masters.

We must search out and allay the anger of many working middle-income Americans burdened by inequitable taxes, unpleasant neighborhoods, and shoddy goods and services.

We shall need to harness the full moral force of our nation to put an end to the most outrageous moral failure of our history—the lingering curse of racism. We must end, too, the blight of hunger, bad housing, and poor health services.

We need most of all to answer the craving of the human

spirit for a sense of belonging, of personal choice, and of pride in family, job, and country.

I offer a public record consistently devoted to these humane values.

I embark on this new journey fully aware both of its glories and of its difficulties. I am sustained by the growing conviction that we have a unique opportunity to redeem this great but troubled land.

I believe the people of this country are tired of the old rhetoric, the unmet promise, the image-makers, and the practitioners of the expedient. The people are not centrist or liberal or conservative. Rather, they seek a way out of the wilderness. But if we who seek their trust, trust them; if we try to evoke the "better angels of our nature," the people will find their own way. We are the children of those who built a great and free nation. And we are no less than that. We must now decide whether our courage and imagination are equal to our talents. If they are, as I believe, then future generations will continue to love America, not simply because it is theirs, but for what it has become—for what, indeed, we have made it.

Press Conference

WASHINGTON, D.C. | JANUARY 19, 1971

Two and a half years ago I asked you to gather in this Capitol to hear my announcement as a candidate for the Democratic presidential nomination. You will recall that I made that announcement only a few days before the 1968 Democratic National Convention in the wake of the tragic death of the late Robert Kennedy. I undertook that last-minute effort at the urging of many of his committed delegates who knew that I deeply shared the twin ideals for which the late Senator Kennedy gave his life—an end to the war in Vietnam and the healing of injustice and trouble in our own land. I am most grateful for the opportunity that brief effort gave me to address the nation in a unique way.

Since 1968, the war in Vietnam has widened into Cambodia and Laos, and a serious economic recession has seized the nation.

Our cities and ghettos seem to be quieter today than they were a few years ago. But it is a stillness born more of resignation and despair than from any confidence in progress or the future. Despite all the discussions, despite the speeches and commissions, the poor remain poor, the oppressed dwell amid their oppression, the environment continues to deteriorate, our rural areas decline, and life in our great cities is steadily dehumanized.

Americans have never believed that simply to talk about problems was to solve them. We need action, and I intend action.

But surely our failure to act must also reflect a larger loss of spirit and confidence—almost as if citizens felt that the conditions and quality of their lives were beyond their influence. And it is this, in my judgment, that is the heart of the matter. From participatory democracy to women's liberation and citizens' conservation councils, we see an increasing assertion of the individual, a desire not simply to have things done, but to do them.

We want to matter as individuals—all of us. The task of future leadership is not to rule people's lives. It is to change the institutions of our society so the citizens may shape their own lives.

I do not intend to assert that these are simple problems or that the answers are obvious. I do know that we must look for new policies and procedures rather than rush to enact new programs which are simply modified versions of old failures. But we cannot begin even this task unless we reverse the growing corruption of public life which views individuals as objects to be deceived or manipulated, and which regards the art of leadership as a capacity to follow the latest public-opinion poll.

I now seek the presidency as a public servant whose career has been devoted from the beginning to the conditions of peace abroad and a humane society at home. I have reached this decision only after a growing conviction that I could bring to the presidency the sense of values, the toughness of mind, and the compassionate spirit which the times demand.

I begin this quest early because I want to travel the land, listening to the concerns and aspirations of the American people and refining my own views on the issues that beset us.

I shall not rely primarily on task-force studies by the experts or on travel to foreign capitals. Rather, I shall make every effort to share a full and honest dialogue with the people of America.

I believe that the American people today want above all else a sense of confidence in themselves and in their leaders. Our people feel a mounting sense of powerlessness to shape their own lives and control their own destiny. The purpose of my candidacy is to assist in the recovery of public confidence and a new pride in our national purpose.

I undertake this quest for the presidency primarily to call the nation home to the liberating ideals that gave us birth.

We need a new dedication to the claims of life over death, to the claims of liberty over oppression, and to the pursuit of happiness over the blight of racism, division, and despair. I know that there is a glorious future for the American people if we are faithful to the ideas of Paine and Madison, of Jefferson and Lincoln.

I do not propose at this time to spell out a detailed blueprint of my positions, but all of you know of my long fight to stop a war in Southeast Asia which has brought such a grievous burden to the American people in the loss of their sons, the inflation of their economy, and the division of their country. I have no doubt that as president, I could end that war quickly on terms that are both acceptable to the American people and in the interest of the suffering peoples of Southeast Asia.

You know, too, that for many years I have called for the

development of conversion planning to divert excessive outlays to the urgent needs of our society.

In the months ahead, I shall be speaking more in depth to the various steps I think our country must take in developing an enlightened foreign policy and a common-sense public agenda here at home.

As for today, let me begin with one pledge above all others— to speak the truth about the hard questions fully and openly.

Victory in Wisconsin

Wisconsin demonstrated the essential soundness of the strategy that was to win the most unlikely presidential nomination in memory.

For more than a year members of my small national staff, some of my few early supporters, and I had been crisscrossing the country on separate routes, finding workers and trying to make my views known. We drew scant national attention. But the reception was favorable at almost every stop. And throughout that year we were building a remarkable campaign organization.

We saw the first fruits of those labors in New Hampshire. I campaigned the state thoroughly, while Senator Muskie, the front runner, was spreading himself thin there and elsewhere. And the thousands of willing workers literally scoured every community for votes. Senator Muskie, from neighboring Maine, was slated to win New Hampshire overwhelmingly. He did win. But his margin—46.4 percent to my 37.1 percent—fell far short of expectations, and my showing convinced the skeptics that we were at last worth watching.

I was in the next primary, in Florida, but we did not expect to do well. My trips there were largely rest stops between grueling campaign tours in New Hampshire and

Wisconsin. And while I was stunned by the size of Governor Wallace's victory, I did not regard my own weak showing as a serious setback. Florida was far more harmful to those who were regarded as the front runners. We were gaining ground, but we were not leading—yet.

Wisconsin was where it happened. That state represented far more than one primary in 1972. I had repeatedly described it as my most crucial test. In fact, it was do or die. Considering the precarious state of our finances, a poor showing there could have forced me out of the race.

We had worked for months to shape what turned out to be a superb campaign structure. Traveling now with a growing press contingent, I campaigned even harder than in New Hampshire. We found out how it sounds in a foundry, how it smells in a tannery (producing leather which would be shipped to New Hampshire to make shoes in the factories we toured there), and finally how it feels to be recognized as a real presidential contender.

Our solid win in Wisconsin was right in line with the scenario we had repeated so many times to disbelieving newsmen and politicians—that by the time of the California primary, it would be a Humphrey-McGovern contest. And after Wisconsin, we could see an open route to the nomination.

So when the returns were in, there was cause for exceptional joy—and also for a new declaration of faith in the principles of our campaign.

MILWAUKEE, WISCONSIN | APRIL 4, 1972

On behalf of my family—and my most devoted campaigner, Eleanor McGovern—thank you for your glorious reception.

I am told that I should be very cautious about claiming too big a victory tonight, lest it suddenly put me in the hazardous position of the front runner.

But I think after a year of adversity, we can stand at least one night of prosperity.

We have won a great victory. It is the first giant step since New Hampshire toward victory in Miami Beach in July—victory over Richard Nixon in November—and finally, the inauguration of a people's president in January.

It is not so much a victory for George McGovern, but a victory for the people—a victory over predictions, polls, and pundits.

Four years ago tonight, Martin Luther King was killed. His life was an affirmation of the founding ideals of this nation—the Declaration of Independence, and the Bill of Rights.

Out of this faith, he testified: "I refuse to accept the view that mankind is so tragically bound to the starless night of racism and war that the bright daylight of peace and brotherhood can never become a reality."

The day Dr. King was struck down, the late Robert Kennedy spoke of his passing. It was only weeks before he himself was to become the victim of senseless violence.

But I believe we can yet achieve the faith of Martin Luther King and the goals the late Robert Kennedy so eagerly sought for us all—"to tame the savageness of man and make gentle the life of the world."

I believe there is a tide running among the American people that we need to seize upon.

It is a tide that would restore truthfulness between the people and their government.

It is a tide that would sweep away the barbarism of war and end the folly of Vietnam.

It is a tide that would end tax favoritism and special privilege for the rich and reduce the burden on the American citizen.

It is a tide that would cleanse the stains of racism, poverty, pollution, drugs, and crime.

I want to strengthen that tide. I want to be able to proclaim in Washington someday that peace has come. I want to be able to proclaim that justice reigns across the land. I want to be able to lead America home to the great ideals that gave birth to this nation.

So, come home, America, to that sense of community that opened our country and gave us nationhood.

For what we need most of all is the assurance that each one of us is a part of a nation where we care about each other.

Let us rededicate our nation to peace and to the healing of our land.

That is the way to leadership for the Democratic Party.

That is the way home for America.

The Acceptance Speech

The McGovern campaign went to Miami with 1,384 delegate votes publicly committed, needing 1,509 for the nomination —close enough, pending a favorable result on the California challenge, to predict a first-ballot victory.

The most obvious source of our strength was our record in the primaries. We won a plurality in ten out of the twenty-three that were held in 1972, and we had at least some delegates in another seven primary states where other candidates came out ahead.

But the margin of victory—nearly 300 committed delegates—came from states where delegates were chosen by caucuses and conventions. Although it was a rare Democratic Party leader who supported me before the Convention, I had a fair chance in those states because, after the bitter 1968 Convention in Chicago, the party rules had been reformed to prohibit closed slate-making and to foster open competition. We had a definite strategy in non-primary states. Thousands of committed local volunteers followed it, producing a succession of minor miracles in 1972. And our delegate total steadily mounted.

Both at and after the Convention, there were suggestions that I had won the nomination because I chaired the commission that wrote the new rules. That experience did help. But it was not because we had any inside knowledge about how the guidelines worked. They were simple, straight-forward, and neutral; they favored no ideology. But while many ignored the reforms, we took them seriously.

A second major factor in setting the stage for the victory at Miami Beach was the most remarkable grass-roots fund-raising in American political history. Scores of generous people conducted a fund-raising campaign that kept us one step ahead of the mounting bills for two years. In fact, we completed the entire journey from the announcement in Sioux Falls to the final election on November 7, 1972, with-out passing on one dollar of indebtedness to the Democratic National Committee—a feat that stands in stunning contrast to the multi-million-dollar deficits of previous presidential campaigns.

It was three A.M. in Miami when I accepted the nomina-tion. Most of the nation was already asleep. The acceptance speech should have been delivered in prime time. But we were told that it would be complicated and against the spirit of reform and openness to change the order of busi-ness or speed the convention along. But it was a mistake. We lost our largest audience of the campaign and our best opportunity to persuade the American people that our reach for fundamental change would help them, not hurt them—that it was rooted in deeply American traditions, and not in some alien radicalism. I wish now, as I did then, that more of the nation had heard the call to come home to our con-stitutional principles; then perhaps that call might have been more widely remembered during the unforeseen diffi-culties just ahead.

MIAMI, FLORIDA | JULY 13, 1972

"Come Home, America"

With a full heart I accept your nomination.

My nomination is all the more precious in that it is the gift of the most open political process in our national history. It is the sweet harvest cultivated by tens of thousands of tireless volunteers—old and young—and funded by literally hundreds of thousands of small contributors. Those who lingered on the edge of despair a brief time ago have been brought into this campaign—heart, hand, head, and soul.

I have been the beneficiary of the most remarkable political organization in American history—an organization that gives dramatic proof to the power of love and to a faith that can move mountains. As Yeats put it: "Count where man's glory most begins and ends, and say my glory was I had such friends."

This is a people's nomination. And next January we will restore the government to the people. American politics will never be the same again.

We are entering a new period of important, hopeful change in America comparable to the political ferment released in the eras of Jefferson, Jackson, and Roosevelt.

I treasure this nomination especially because it comes after vigorous competition with the ablest men and women our party can offer: my old and treasured friend and neighbor, Hubert Humphrey; that gracious and good man from Maine, Ed Muskie; a tough fighter for his beliefs, Scoop Jackson; a brave and spirited woman, Shirley Chisholm; a wise and powerful lawmaker from Arkansas, Wilbur Mills; the man from North Carolina who opened new vistas in education and public excellence, Terry Sanford; the leader who in 1968 combined the travail and the hope of the American spirit, Gene McCarthy.

And I was as moved as all of you by the appearance at this convention of the governor of Alabama, George Wallace. His votes in the primaries showed the depth of discontent in this country, and his courage in the face of pain and adversity is the mark of a man of boundless will. We all despise the senseless act that disrupted his campaign. Governor, we pray for your speedy and full recovery, so you can stand up and speak out forcefully for all of those who see you as their champion.

In the months ahead, I covet the help of every Democrat and every Republican and independent who wants America to be the great and good land it can be.

This is going to be a national campaign carried to every part of the nation—north, south, east, and west. We are not conceding a single state to Richard Nixon. I want to say to my friend, Frank King, that Ohio may have passed a few times at this convention but *I'm* not going to pass Ohio. Governor Gilligan, Ohio may be a little slow counting the votes, but when they come in this November, they are going to show a Democratic victory.

To anyone in this hall or beyond who doubts the ability of Democrats to join together in common cause, I say never underestimate the power of Richard Nixon to bring harmony to Democratic ranks. He is our unwitting unifier and the fundamental issue of this campaign. And all of us together are going to help him redeem the pledge he made ten years ago: Next year you won't have Richard Nixon to kick around any more.

We have had our fury and our frustrations in these past months and at this convention.

Well, I frankly welcome the contrast with the smug, dull, and empty event which will take place here in Miami next month. We chose this struggle. We reformed our party and let the people in.

And we stand today not as a collection of back-room strategists, not as a tool of ITT or any other special interest, but as a direct reflection of the public will.

So let our opponents stand on the status quo, while we seek to refresh the American spirit.

Let the opposition collect their $10 million in secret money from the privileged. And let us find one million ordinary Americans who will contribute $25 each to this campaign—"A Million-Member Club" with members who will expect, not special favors for themselves, but a better land for us all.

In Scripture and in the music of our children we are told: "To everything there is a season, and a time to every purpose under heaven."

And for America, the time has come at last.

This is the time for truth, not falsehood.

In a democratic nation, no one likes to say that his inspiration came from secret arrangements behind closed doors. But in a sense that is how my candidacy began. I am here as your candidate tonight in large part because during four administrations of both parties, a terrible war has been charted behind closed doors.

I want those doors opened, and I want that war closed. And I make these pledges above all others—the doors of government will be opened, and that brutal war will be closed.

Truth is a habit of integrity, not a strategy of politics. And if we nurture the habit of truth in this campaign, we will continue to be truthful once we are in the White House. Let us say to Americans, as Woodrow Wilson said in his first campaign: " . . . let me inside (the government) and I will tell you everything that is going on in there."

The destiny of America is safer in the hands of the people than in the conference rooms of any elite. Let us give our country the chance to elect a government that will seek and speak the truth, for this is a time for truth in the life of our nation.

And this is a time, not for death, but for life.

In 1968, Americans voted to bring our sons home from Vietnam in peace—and since then, twenty thousand have come home in coffins.

I have no secret plan for peace. I have a public plan.

As one whose heart has ached for ten years over the agony of Vietnam, I will halt the senseless bombing of Indochina on Inauguration Day.

There will be no more Asian children running ablaze from bombed-out schools.

There will be no more talk of bombing the dikes or the cities of the north.

Within ninety days of my inauguration, every American soldier and every American prisoner will be out of the jungle and out of their cells and back home in America where they belong.

And then let us resolve that never again will we shed the precious young blood of this nation to prop up a cruel and corrupt dictatorship ten thousand miles from our shores.

Let us choose life, not death. This is the time.

This is also the time to turn away from excessive preoccupation overseas to rebuilding our own nation.

America must be restored to her proper role in the world. But we can do that only through the recovery of confidence in ourselves. The greatest contribution America can make to our fellow mortals is to heal our own great but deeply troubled land. We must respond to that ancient command: "Physician, heal thyself."

It is necessary in an age of nuclear power and hostile ideologies that we be militarily strong. America must never become a second-rate nation. As one who has tasted the bitter fruits of our weakness before Pearl Harbor, 1941, I give you my sacred pledge that if I become president of the United States, America will keep its defenses alert and fully sufficient to meet any danger. We will do that not only for ourselves, but for those who deserve and need the shield of our strength—our old allies in Europe and elsewhere, including the people of Israel, who will always have our help to hold their promised land.

Yet we know that for thirty years we have been so absorbed with fear and danger from abroad that we have permitted our own house to fall into disarray. We must now show that peace and prosperity can exist side by side—indeed, each now depends on the other.

National strength includes the credibility of our system in the eyes of our own people as well as the credibility of our deterrent in the eyes of others abroad. National security includes schools for our children as well as silos for our missiles, the health of our families as much as the size of our bombs, the safety of our streets and the condition of our cities and not just the engines of war. And if we someday choke on the pollution of our own air, there will be little consolation in leaving behind a dying continent ringed with steel.

So while protecting ourselves abroad let us "form a more perfect union" here at home. This is the time.

And we must make this a time of justice and jobs for all.

For more than three years, we have tolerated stagnation and a rising level of joblessness, with more than five million of our best workers unemployed. Surely this is the most false and wasteful economics. Our deep need is not for idleness, but for new housing and hospitals, for facilities to combat pollution and take us home from work, for products better able to compete on vigorous world markets.

The highest domestic priority of my administration will be to ensure that every American able to work has a job to do. This job guarantee will and must depend upon a reinvigorated private economy, freed at last from the uncertainties and burdens of war. But it is our commitment that whatever employment the private sector does not provide, the federal government will either stimulate, or provide itself. Whatever it takes, this country is going back to work.

America cannot exist with most of our people working and paying taxes, to support too many others mired in a hopeless welfare mess. Therefore, we intend to begin by putting millions back to work; and after that is done, we will assure to those unable to work an income adequate to a decent life.

Beyond this, a program to put America back to work demands that work be properly rewarded. That means the end of a system of economic controls in which labor is depressed, but prices and corporate profits run sky-high. It means a system of national health insurance, so that a worker can afford decent health care for himself and his family. It means real enforcement of the laws so that the drug racketeers are put behind bars for good and our streets are once again safe for our families.

Above all, honest work must be rewarded by a fair and just tax system. The tax system today does not reward hard work; it penalizes it. Inherited or invested wealth frequently multiplies itself while paying no taxes at all. But wages earned on the assembly line, or farming the land—these hard-earned dollars are taxed to the last penny. There is a depletion allowance for oil wells, but no allowance for depleting the farmer who feeds us or the worker who serves us all.

The Administration tells us that we should not discuss tax

reform in an election year. They would prefer to keep all discussion of the tax laws in closed rooms, where they, their powerful friends, and their paid lobbyists can turn every effort at reform into a new loophole for the rich. But an election year is the people's year to speak; and this year, the people are going to ensure that the tax system is changed so that work is rewarded and so that those who derive the highest benefits will pay their fair share rather than slipping through the loopholes at the expense of the rest of us.

So let us stand for justice, and jobs, and against special privilege. This is the time.

We are not content with things as they are. We reject the view of those who say: "America—love it or leave it." We reply: "Let us change America, so we can love it the more."

And this is the time. It is the time for this land to become again a witness to the world for what is noble and just in human affairs. It is the time to live more with faith and less with fear—with an abiding confidence that can sweep away the strongest barriers between us and teach us that we truly are brothers and sisters.

So join with me in this campaign. Lend me your strength and your support—and together, we will call America home to the ideals that nourished us in the beginning.

From secrecy, and deception in high places, come home, America.

From a conflict in Indochina which maims our ideals as well as our soldiers, come home, America.

From military spending so wasteful that it weakens our nation, come home, America.

From the entrenchment of special privilege and tax favoritism—

From the waste of idle hands to the joy of useful labor—

From the prejudice of race and sex—

From the loneliness of the aging poor and the despair of the neglected sick, come home, America.

Come home to the affirmation that we have a dream.

Come home to the conviction that we can move our country forward.

Come home to the belief that we can seek a newer world.

And let us be joyful in the homecoming. For:

"This land is your land, this land is my land.

"From California to the New York Island,

"From the redwood forests to the Gulf Stream waters.

"This land was made for you and me."

May God grant us the wisdom to cherish this good land, and to meet the great challenge that beckons us home.

This is the time.

The Second Convention

In the wake of revelations about his long history of mental illness, Senator Eagleton had resigned as our vice-presidential candidate. And through the process of affirming my confidence in him so we could have a fair test of the public reaction to these belated disclosures, then doubting the wisdom of his continuing, and finally concluding that it would be necessary for him to leave the ticket, I had lost the impression of constancy which had been among my greatest assets in the campaign until then.

Within a week, Sargent Shriver was chosen to replace Senator Eagleton. I addressed the meeting of the National Committee which ratified the Shriver selection, and through the fall Ambassador Shriver amply vindicated what I said of him that night. He did bring a special strength and faith to our struggle. And at this "second convention" the campaign found a renewal of faith in itself.

Democratic National Committee Convention for the Selection of A Vice-Presidential Nominee

AUGUST 8, 1972

We meet tonight to restore the hope of victory and the dream of a better land.

We meet in the wake of hard and painful weeks, but we feel no despair, no loss of direction, no lack of purpose.

We have dreamed a great dream—we have fought from New Hampshire to Miami—and we will not rest until we reach the promised land.

So we begin our campaign anew, with the conviction that it will end in victory.

Tonight, we recall the words of Thomas Paine: "I love the man that can smile in trouble, that can gather strength from distress, and grow brave by reflection."

And from the trial through which we have passed, we gather strength for the task that is before us.

We gather strength from the tribulation of Tom Eagleton—who forfeited his place on the ticket to advance other hopes for the country.

We gather strength from the choice of Sargent Shriver—who inspires us with his contagious faith that our cause will prevail, and whose years of service bear eloquent witness to the ideals we share and seek for America's future.

Sargent Shriver sent the Peace Corps around the world; and in the next administration, America will send forth once more the message of peace on earth.

Sargent Shriver commanded the war on poverty; and in the next administration, that is the war America will wage and win.

And if we have used valuable time in the selection of a vice-presidential nominee, the nation must wish the Republicans had made their choice with greater care.

Most of all, we gather strength from the knowledge that, despite the difficulties of the moment, we have the opportunity of a generation to give the government of America back to the people of America. We have within our grasp the power to reclaim the nation our forebears left us, so that freedom can truly ring again.

For freedom is in doubt when a child cries out in hunger, when a man calls a hovel his home, when the sick are neglected, and the aged are abandoned, and millions of willing hands are without work.

And when the government lies, the people lose their liberty.

A campaign promise is a debt to the people—and the Nixon Administration is in a state of bankruptcy. Their only answer to our problems is to echo their broken promises of 1968.

They are promising once again an end to the fighting in Vietnam. Would you believe that promise from those politicians who have sacrificed another twenty thousand of our sons since they were elected on a pledge to end the war?

They are repeating their promise to stop inflation and create jobs. Would you believe that promise from those politicians who have thrown another two million people out of work and practiced their own campaign rhetoric about runaway inflation?

They are promising, as they did before, to make our streets safe for our citizens. Would you believe that promise from those politicians who have permitted our national Democratic headquarters to be bugged and invaded under circumstances that point strongly toward Mr. Nixon's campaign management?

Indeed, we may fairly ask: Would anyone who remembers the course of the last four years believe any promise from these Republican politicians?

But they think they can make America believe in their broken promises by making the American people afraid.

They are telling the country that the Democratic Party is the party of radicalism. But what is right has always been called radical by those with a stake in things that are wrong.

In 1932, a Republican president called Franklin Roosevelt's economic policy "the fumes of the . . . cauldron which boiled in Russia." Franklin Roosevelt won the election.

In 1948, a Republican senator charged that Harry Truman's "program would create a nation completely regimented, choked by taxation, under the complete domination of arbitrary union leadership." Harry Truman won the election.

In 1960, a Republican writer said that John Kennedy would "imperil our freedom in order to promote expensive socialistic enterprises." John Kennedy won the election.

Now, in 1972, the Republican scare tactic is that we are radical. And we will win the election.

The American people are smarter than the Nixon strategists. They will listen in the fall as they listened in the spring. And we will listen to them.

The American people will learn that we want for the country only what they want for themselves—a chance to enrich this brief span of human life through the energy, the skill, and the strength of the society their ancestors created and they now sustain.

So the mission of the Democratic Party is not radicalism, but the restoration of America's ancient values.

To those who have borne the weight of senseless war, we will restore the blessings of peace.

And we will resolve never again to commit the young life of America to the defense of a corrupt dictator half a world away.

We will beat at least some of the swords of war into plowshares of peace.

Let us create public transportation for people instead of more destruction of the dikes and rice paddies of Vietnam. Let us have smarter children instead of smarter bombs. Let us save cities in America instead of destroying villages in Vietnam.

Then, perhaps, we can start to teach a battered and bloodstained world the truth of these words: "The human race is a family. Men are brothers. All wars are civil wars. All killing is fratricidal. And peace is a condition of survival."

And this, too, is our pledge: To the millions who have seen their work disappear or the rewards of work decline, we will restore the justice of jobs and the worth of wages. By shifting excessive military spending to wiser and more urgent uses, we will multiply the total demand for brains and hands. And we will assure every worker that there will be work to do—and that prices will not soar while wages fall. Whatever it takes, this country will return to full employment.

And to the many who are deprived, while there is special protection for the few, we will restore the equality of rights that is at the heart of our national heritage.

The opposition has now collected $10 million in secret money from the privileged—money which they refuse to disclose to public view. We do not have a secret fund of millions given by the few. But we ask tonight that millions of Americans contribute what they can to launch this campaign for the people.

Let the opposition look after the interests of executives in corporate board rooms. We will serve the interests of Americans on the assembly line, on the farm, and up and down the main streets of America.

We will fight for a fair and just tax system so that workers will no longer be taxed more heavily than the wealthy. We will fight to assure a living income to all our people.

And do not believe it when they tell you that average Americans will have to pay the bill. That is a lie. We can raise every citizen above the poverty level without raising the taxes of any family that lives on wages or a salary. Instead, the bill will be paid by those who now slip through loopholes at the expense of the rest of us. The bill will be paid by ending the waste and fat in a demoralized military establishment that needs to be streamlined and revitalized.

This year, we seek a government without secret money, secret plans, or secret deals.

This year, we seek the kind of government that was the gift of the first Americans to every generation of Americans.

We seek to take up the journey of our grandparents and their parents before them. That journey started with a little band of pilgrims on the edge of a hostile continent. It was swelled by millions of immigrants who spread across the land until they truly reached from sea to shining sea.

Robert Frost once wrote: "What makes a country in the beginning is a good piece of geography."

But what finally made our country great was its people and the splendor of their ideals.

So it is time for a new American journey—not to an alien ideology or a foreign conflict, but home to the spirit which gave us freedom and nationhood. It is time for all of us to say: "Come home, America."

In the pain and anguish of the last decade, our people have looked for light in the gathering darkness. In 1972, we will decide whether the shadows will continue to close in, or whether America will again lift the light of decency and compassion before the world.

So, my fellow citizens, this is what I ask of you:

Vote for the prisoner of war who cannot vote—so that he may be free.

Vote for the people of Southeast Asia who have no voice—so that they may live.

Vote for the workers without work and the families without food—so that they may prosper.

And vote for yourselves, for your right to live in justice and peace—so that you may receive the fullness of America's promise.

During the presidential election of 1860, with the nation on the brink of civil conflict, Abraham Lincoln wrote a friend a letter often quoted by the late President Kennedy: "I know there is a God and that He hates injustice. I see the storm coming, but if He has a place and a part for me, I believe that I am ready."

Now, over a century later, when the great issue is restoring peace and justice to our land once again, we know there is a God and we know He hates injustice, and we see the storm coming. But if He has a place for us, let us be ready.

Labor Day:
The Traditional Opening

Of necessity, I had sought the nomination as if there were no tomorrow. I was tired and numb from campaigning almost without letup for eighteen months. So we scheduled some time at Sylvan Lake Lodge in Custer, South Dakota, to rest and to plan for the fall campaign against Mr. Nixon.

Our other pressing task was to reassure those traditional sources of Democratic support who had doubts about my candidacy. We had to repair some of the damage done in hard-fought primaries, particularly in Nebraska, Ohio, and California, and in divisive post-primary battles. The groundless "three A's" charge (that I favored acid, amnesty, and abortion), first voiced by Republican Senate Leader Hugh Scott, had been picked up and repeated effectively by some of our Democratic opponents. Doubts had been falsely raised about my support for Israel. And a number of individuals who had traditionally exerted great influence in the party had taken my victory as a personal affront. So the August schedule included speeches to labor audiences, leaders in the Jewish community, veterans, and educators. It included a visit to the Johnson Ranch in Texas, a meeting with Southern governors, a discussion with senior citizens' representatives in Washington, and a scheduled talk at the Illinois State Fair with Chicago's Mayor Richard Daley, whose delegation had been unseated in Miami. (Mayor Daley did not come to the meeting, but he eventually gave his strong and effective support to the ticket.)

We were not particularly successful, either at resting ourselves or restoring the party. The Eagleton trauma disrupted the relative serenity at Sylvan Lake, and that fast-breaking story—not the olive branches and reassuring words—also became the biggest news and the dominant campaign preoccupation for most of the month of August.

But Labor Day always marks the opening of Democratic campaigns, and suddenly Labor Day was upon us. Many of the traditional events—like the famous rally in Detroit's Cadillac Square—have been discontinued. Two that retain their vitality and enthusiasm are in northern Ohio, and there is another in Alameda County, California. I spoke at all three with an emphasis on economic issues, especially tax reform. I suspect that the attack launched in these speeches against a national sales tax—the so-called "value added tax"—had something to do with the Administration's about-face decision to repudiate that scheme not long afterwards. My message on Labor Day was basic. I attempted to continue the post-Convention unity effort by pointing out that whether the issue was taxes, or jobs, or war and peace, the Democratic Party was, as it always had been, the real tribune of working men and women.

BARBERTON AND CHIPPEWA LAKE, OHIO
ALAMEDA COUNTY, CALIFORNIA | SEPTEMBER 4, 1972

We are here to celebrate the holiday of those who earn their living the hard way—with sweat and strength, with the skill of their hands and the pride of honest labor.

We are also here because we are determined to end another holiday—the long, involuntary holiday of five million workers who have been unemployed under Richard Nixon.

We are here to say that this nation belongs to the people

who build and support it, not to a handful of executives in the board rooms of corporate power and the back rooms of the White House.

We are here because we believe that workers are not robots, to be run at the flick of a management switch—but free human beings with an inalienable right to dignity, safety, and security.

In the last eighteen months, I have walked through countless factories, and I have seen monotony and danger on too many assembly lines.

I have seen assembly lines where men are treated as machines whose only purpose is to supply a weld, a rivet, or a stitch. I have seen assembly lines which mean not only products for consumers, but endless, grinding boredom for workers.

I have spoken to workers who can barely hear because their ears have been deadened by the pounding of metal.

I have talked with workers who gasp as they breathe because management put a lid on their factory and locked the pollution inside.

I have met workers who will never work again because big business cut corners on job safety.

Now I would like Richard Nixon to come out of the White House—not to listen to the push-button praises of a stage-managed convention, but to listen to grievances at a plant gate.

Then let him tell us that we cannot afford enough safety inspectors to stop the slaughter in industry and mining.

Then let him tell us that the country cannot work for you, as you have worked for the country.

And we will reply with a campaign that will add two more names to the unemployment rolls in November—Richard Nixon and Spiro Agnew.

I am here because this is the time and place to begin that campaign—among working men and women on Labor Day.

No political party can serve two masters—the people and the privileged. By heritage and by choice, this is the fundamental difference between the Democratic Party and the Republican Party.

The Democratic Party is the party of the people. The Republican Party is the party of the privileged. And this election is the renewal of a struggle as old as the Great Depression, and as recent as the economic black magic invented by Richard Nixon when he gave us recession and inflation at the same time.

Last month, Mr. Nixon announced that our party had deserted its principles, and he called on Democrats to join him in a "new majority." The slogan is new, but the strategy is exactly the same as the Nixon attack on John Kennedy. Listen to Mr. Nixon's words in 1960:

"I say that those who adopted the Democratic platform in Los Angeles have forfeited the right to ask millions of Democrats to be loyal to their party and to vote the Democratic ticket."

This was pompous nonsense in 1960—and it is pompous nonsense now.

Most Democrats refused to desert John Kennedy—and they will not desert the McGovern-Shriver ticket.

Of course, there is a group called Democrats for Nixon, run by John Connally, who recently said that today's tax loopholes are fair and that full employment is a myth.

The Republicans are welcome to Mr. Connally and his exclusive club of oil millionaires. I want the oil workers, the steelworkers, the machinists, the teachers, and millions of other Americans who live on the wages of their work instead of tax loopholes.

The only way the President can achieve a new majority in this election is to trick the vast majority of the voters. So just as he tried to do when John Kennedy was the Democratic nominee, Richard Nixon is now trying to make the nation fear the Democrats.

He is trying to make people afraid that Democrats are extremists, who want to tax too much and spend more than we have. But that is the oldest lie in the reactionary Republican book of partisan smears. And just because the election comes a week after Halloween is no excuse to use the campaign as a time to scare the country.

So let us separate fact from fear and look at the real choice before the country.

The real choice is four more years of secret plans to end the war, or an open plan to bring our sons home from the jungles and the jails of Indochina.

The real choice is four more years of unemployment, or four years of peacetime prosperity.

And when that choice becomes clear, it will not be the American people but Richard Nixon who has something to fear in 1972.

John Connally may think full employment is a myth; I think it is a necessity. Our highest economic priority is the lowest possible unemployment.

Richard Nixon has vetoed four bills to create jobs. As president, I will sign those bills. Whatever it takes, we will guarantee a job opportunity to every man and woman in America who is able to work.

That is the McGovern position. The Nixon policy calls for joblessness instead of jobs.

And once this difference becomes clear, it will not be the American people but Richard Nixon who has something to fear.

The real choice in this election is also between four more years of inflation and four years of stable prices.

Whenever you shop at the local grocery store, you find out that Richard Nixon costs more. He says he stands for the value of the dollar—but consumer prices have risen eighteen points while he has been in power. The Nixon inflation is ground into every pound of hamburger you buy.

The President says inflation is under control. I say let him try to feed his family for a week on an average pay check.

The Nixon policy puts no controls on the dividends and profits of the special interests, because they have a friend in the White House. As president, I will adopt an even-handed policy to stop inflation—and the corporations and the rich will bear the burden, too.

That is the difference between the McGovern position and the Nixon position.

And once that difference becomes clear, it will not be the American people but Richard Nixon who has something to fear in 1972.

And perhaps the most important choice in this election is the choice between tax favoritism and tax justice.

Last week I went to Wall Street and told the truth about our tax system.

I said it was wrong to impose taxes in bold print and then to give them back in the fine print to a favored few.

I said that it was wrong to allow an American with an income of $2,300,000 to pay taxes at less than half the rate you pay on the first $1,000 of your taxable earnings.

It is wrong that ITT pays taxes at a rate of 5 percent, and Texaco pays at a rate of 3 percent, while you pay what the tax tables say.

And it is wrong that some wealthy Americans escape taxes by spending more to hire a tax lawyer than most Americans make in an entire year.

The Republicans say I want to soak the rich. I want the rich and the corporations to pay their fair share and no more. And what I really want is to stop soaking rank-and-file taxpayers.

You pay for every tax loophole. You pay for every martini lunch that a businessman deducts while you eat a bologna sandwich. You pay every dime the oil companies do not pay. You pay half the tax on the increased value of a corporate executive's stocks and bonds.

Money made by money should be taxed at the same rate as money made by men. Tax justice demands equal treatment for Americans who earn their living at a lathe and Americans who collect their dividends in the mail.

I have demanded a program to close $22 billion in tax loopholes. It will not take one extra cent from any American whose income comes from wages or salaries, or from investments that are already fairly taxed. None of you will pay more—but corporations and the wealthy will finally pay what they owe to their country.

With the money we raise from tax reform, we can afford $15 billion for aid to local schools and for substantial property tax reduction. Then we can assure a good education for our children without the insecurity of higher property taxes for their parents.

Richard Nixon also has a plan for your taxes. It is a secret plan—the same kind of plan he promised for peace in Vietnam four years ago. And I think this time the secret plan is not to reduce your taxes, but to raise them.

If Mr. Nixon is reelected—a prospect I seldom dwell upon— I predict that he will call for higher taxes in the form of a national sales tax. This Nixon sales tax would leave the loopholes wide open, but it would hit hardest at the working class, the poor, older people, and middle-income families.

To take the sting out the President will call it a value added tax. But a sales tax by any other name smells the same.

The McGovern answer is $22 billion in tax reform, and $15 billion for quality education and property tax relief, so that you will pay less.

And when this difference becomes clear, it will not be the American people but Richard Nixon who has something to fear in 1972.

These are the choices I will take to the American people. I ask your help in that effort.

I have no secret $10 million fund from those who want special favors for themselves. I have no secret fund at all, for we have disclosed every single dime raised and spent in this campaign. But what I am looking for is a million Americans who will contribute $25 each, or whatever they can afford, because they want a better land for us all.

That is how we will run a people's campaign. We will operate differently from the Committee to Re-Elect the President.

The Committee to Re-Elect the President has become the Committee to Protect the Special Interests. And their only defense is to cover up their failures by shouting that the Democrats are radical.

But what is right has always been called radical by those with a stake in things that are wrong.

The robber barons called unions radical when they organized the docks of San Francisco, the factories of Cleveland, and the coal mines of Pennsylvania. But justice on the job wasn't radical then, and it isn't radical now.

What is really radical is an administration that has turned your government into the White House–Wall Street connection. In the words of Franklin Roosevelt, "The economic royalists complain that we seek to overthrow the institutions of America. What they really complain of is that we seek to take away their power."

I was a bomber pilot in World War Two. And I still remember the day when we were hit so hard over Germany that we were all ready to bail out. I want to tell you I was scared, but I thought we could make it back. So I gave this order to the crew: "Resume your stations, we're going to bring this plane home."

We have had a difficult and trying month. But on this Labor Day, I say to you and to workers across America, to Democrats who are fainthearted and to those who are anxious to fight on, and to people everywhere who share our cause: "Resume your stations, we're going to bring America home."

The Concession:
A Journey Ends

Someone has written of the "sting of defeat." But a landslide defeat in politics does not sting. It aches. It builds with each memory and with each thought of what might have been done differently—with every recollection of the breaks and mistakes that have so much to do with the fortunes of politicians. The ache subsides slowly. And despite the determination to be brave, there certainly were some tears to be shed in the weeks after November 7, 1972.

Under ordinary circumstances a presidential campaign of the kind we waged would be physically impossible. After it was over, United Airlines—the supplier of the two aircraft we chartered from Labor Day on—sent us a chart of the "George McGovern Presidential Campaign Tour, 1972." It has our routes drawn on a map of the United States, looking like a big spider web—skewed toward the major industrial states we felt we had to win. It shows one hundred and thirty flights between Labor Day and the election, and more than fifty thousand miles of travel. It does not show all the other miles by car and bus caravan; the speeches to hundreds of rallies at airports, city intersections, and hotel ballrooms; the long hours of meetings with local workers and dignitaries; the missed or hurried meals and the late nights spent working over the next day's speeches; the press conferences, telethons, and interviews; or all the other elements that drain every reserve of energy from the candidate, his staff, and the traveling press. It can only be survived through the restorative effects of huge, enthusiastic crowds; through the recognition that hundreds of thousands of people are working hard in communities across the land; and, finally, through the knowledge that, one way or another, it will certainly end on the appointed day.

Just a few campaigns ago, on the day before the election, a candidate was lucky to cover several hundred miles in a single region, usually the Northeast. In 1972 on that last day we had covered 5,000 miles—from New York to Philadelphia to Wichita to Southern California and finally home in South Dakota. I was already resigned to what seemed inevitable; the polls were discouraging; the predictions were pessimistic; and the press was already preparing its analysis of the defeat. . . .

The time to concede came earlier than we expected. I worked over this statement with a fading felt-tipped pen, using my bed for a desk. It describes better than anything I could say now what I felt was important on that disappointing evening.

SIOUX FALLS, SOUTH DAKOTA | NOVEMBER 7, 1972

Here among my friends in South Dakota where this campaign began almost twenty-three months ago, we now bring it to an end tonight. I have just sent the following telegram to President Nixon:

"Congratulations on your victory. I hope that in the next four years you will lead us to a time of peace abroad and justice at home. You have my full support in such efforts. With best wishes to you and your gracious wife, Pat. Sincerely, George McGovern."

The first presidential concession that I remember hearing was that of Adlai Stevenson in 1952. He recalled the old Lincoln story of the boy who had stubbed his toe in the dark and when the lad was asked how it felt, he replied, "Well, it hurts too much to laugh, but I'm too old to cry."

It does hurt all of us in this auditorium and many others across the country to lose, but we are not going to shed any tears tonight about the great joys that this campaign has brought to us over the past two years. All of the satisfaction and joy that we have found in these past twenty-two months are not going to be washed away with the tears and regrets of one night.

We have found the greatest outpouring of energy and love that any political effort has ever inspired, at least in my lifetime. Eleanor and I and our family, along with Sargent and Eunice Shriver, will never forget the people of this campaign. We will never forget those that we have seen in countless meeting places all across this country, those we knew about on the telephone and on their feet, who have worked so hard, so terribly hard, for all these many, many long months.

The poet Yeats said something that I quoted the night of the Massachusetts primary—and it looks like Massachusetts is coming through again tonight. Yeats said, "Count where man's glory most begins and ends, and say my glory was I had such friends." And that is the way I feel tonight.

The presidency belongs to someone else. But the glory of these devoted working friends, and their dedication to the noble ideals of this country, sustains us now and it will sustain our country. We will shed no tears because all of this effort will bear fruit for years to come.

There can be no question at all that we have pushed this country in the direction of peace, and I think each of us loves the title of peacemaker more than any office in the land. We will press on with that effort until all the bloodshed and all the sorrow have ended once and for all.

I want every single one of you to remember, and never forget it, that if we pushed the day of peace just one day closer, then every minute and every hour and every bone-crushing effort in this campaign was worth the entire sacrifice.

And if we have brought into the political process those who never before have experienced either its joy or its sorrows, then that too is an enduring blessing.

Now the question is, to what standard does the loyal opposition now rally? We do not rally to the support of policies that we deplore. But we do love this country and we will continue to beckon it to a higher standard.

So I ask all of you tonight to stand with your convictions. I ask you not to despair at the political process of this country because that process has yielded so much valuable improvement in these past two years. The Democratic Party will be a better party because of the reforms that we have carried out. The nation will be better because we never once gave up the long battle to renew its oldest ideals and to redirect its current energies along more humane and hopeful paths.

So let us play the proper role of the loyal opposition, and let us play it in those familiar words from Isaiah that I have quoted so frequently: "They that wait upon the Lord shall renew their strength; they shall mount up with wings as eagles; they shall run, and not be weary; they shall walk, and not faint."

God bless you. Good night.

DESTINATIONS

During the campaign I made speeches, issued statements or position papers, and responded to questions on literally dozens of issues. We wanted to have an answer to every group and even every individual who wrote asking my views on issues that were their special concerns. In both campaigns, for the nomination and for the presidency, I answered questions not only from the press but from the general public, in question-and-answer sessions and in live telethons. (In light of later revelations, I suppose we also answered questions asked by a good many of Mr. Nixon's campaign agents representing themselves as concerned citizens—debating his bottom-level hirelings, in effect, while he personally spurned debates and tried to ignore the fact that there even was such a thing as a campaign going on.) I also delivered major addresses on such issues as crime, housing and urban problems, antitrust and monopoly power, agriculture, energy and the environment, foreign policy, women's rights, civil rights, the United Nations, and many others. I did see it as an ideological campaign. I thought the philosophy and the priorities I represented were much more in keeping with the mood and the needs of the country than were the policies of the Nixon Administration. And I wanted to be as comprehensive as possible in setting forth an alternative American agenda.

Yet it is impossible to run a campaign on every issue. It would leave the electorate with a blurred image, when what is really needed is a clear understanding of what the candidate sees as the nation's overriding concerns and a public sense of how he would approach them. So, while some supporters felt we should focus more on the issues that had drawn them personally to the campaign, I tried to concentrate on four broad areas that I felt could inspire a majority of the American people. I spoke most frequently and in the most detail about the Indochina war, the issue which made my candidacy possible; corruption, including the unprecedented corruption of the political process; the economy, including tax reform; and the need to reorder national priorities, to scale down excessive military spending and convert the economy to works of peace.

Even with this narrowing we may have tried to develop too many issues. Each of the four broad areas encompasses a host of subareas which, in turn, deserved comment. It could well have been better campaign strategy to narrow still further. But in retrospect it probably would not have made a difference in the outcome. And I do feel that by addressing these questions in depth, we made a contribution to the American political dialogue that will last well beyond 1972. The issues and these answers will remain vital for years to come.

Let the Sunshine In

Political manipulation of information, the distortion of truth, is not necessarily a violation of law. But it does violate the needs of a system of self-government. From the time this paper was released ahead of the New Hampshire primary campaign we concentrated on its timely open-politics provisions. We found a favorable public response there to my unilateral disclosure of personal finances and of campaign finances *before* the law required it. The call for debates was finally heeded in New Hampshire, then never again until the California primary, and then never at all in the fall.

In the aftermath, calculating the effect of open campaigning, I find myself still troubled. I believe openness is a worthy and essential standard of political conduct. Yet I also believe it hurt us badly. I do not blame the press covering my campaign. Like all politicians, I was irked and angered by news accounts and columns I thought were unfair. But I think the coverage of our side of the race was generally fair and reasonable.

Yet at the same time Mr. Nixon ran a closed and carefully manipulated operation, backed up by the inherent power of the presidency to control events and, therefore, the news. So in 1972, "balanced" political reporting meant covering my faults and foibles as well as my stands because there was access, and then giving equal time and space to some thirty Republican surrogates who were not running for anything and usually had never been elected to anything, as they hustled around the country singing praises to their White House boss and benefactor.

Under these circumstances our open approach had become a strategic drawback. Yet we could not waver from it, for fear of being termed hypocritical. Reporters covering the Democratic campaign had grown accustomed to our approach and would write harshly about any variation; those covering the Republican campaign were used to denials, lies, and silence, to hard news that was exclusively self-serving, so they seldom complained—at least in print. As we learned only later, Mr. Nixon did not excel at choosing or managing a staff, and he was certainly not adept at picking a vice-presidential candidate. But his coverup worked, at least long enough to keep him in office. Our every error was spotlighted.

Yet I am unshaken in the view that the open approach to campaigning, and the more important steps to open the operations of government to public scrutiny, are fundamental if democracy itself is to have real meaning. Perhaps one helpful step would be for the newspapers, news services, and networks to rotate their political correspondents back and forth between the candidates so they could better measure the differences. But in any case, we are left to find ways of assuring true balance, so that candor, and not camouflage, will reap some of the rewards.

WASHINGTON, D.C. | DECEMBER 23, 1971

The need to restore public trust in government is among the most urgent challenges confronting the country as we move into the 1972 election year.

Opinion surveys in recent years have consistently shown that confidence in government has fallen to all-time lows—that many Americans have begun to doubt or disbelieve virtually everything they are told by politicians and public officials, and to believe that government exists not to serve the needs of the people but simply to preserve its own power.

The sources of public suspicion and alienation are not hard to find. Put bluntly, government is not believed because it has not been leveling with the people.

The gap between pre-election promise and post-election performance has grown to a chasm in recent years, in nearly every area of public concern from war and peace to law and order. Political campaigns have degenerated into contests between polling techniques and advertising agencies, to see who is best at packaging candidates and manipulating public opinion.

The same approach continues after Election Day. The White House staff has more public-relations experts today than at any time in history, and the sale of Administration policies has become a major bureaucratic preoccupation. Meanwhile the President isolates himself from hard questions by holding fewer presidential press conferences than any of his predecessors, and by demanding network television time so he can speak without the risk of challenge.

Objective reporting has been further chilled by unprecedented harassment of the press—including attempted prior restraints, threatened retaliation for unfavorable reporting and commentary, and even an FBI investigation of a network newsman.

Sources of reliable statistical information are also declining. Expert background briefings on the economy were ended, and reports on urban unemployment were canceled, because they contradicted the Administration's own self-serving descriptions. Crime reports are filtered through political appointees, to make the Administration's record look better, before they reach the press and the public. The parity reporting system for agriculture was changed because the figures exposed an embarrassing contrast between Candidate Nixon's promises and President Nixon's result on farm prices.

Even the Administration's use of language inspires disbelief. We have a "jobs" program which is, in reality, a $9 billion tax giveaway for big business; a "revolution" which is, in truth, a scheme to reshuffle the bureaucracy; a "finest hour" which is, in fact, the abysmal national tragedy in Indochina.

The Nixon Administration is without peer in its efforts to mislead the American people. But it does not have a monopoly. The Pentagon papers disclose a long pattern of deliberate deception and contrivance on the most profound issues of the decade.

Meanwhile, responsible officials have hidden their doubts about the war in Vietnam, and have withheld their honest judgments from the public while at the same time professing consistent public support for a disastrous policy.

An informed electorate is a primary condition of democracy. It follows that the deceptive practices of recent years, while they create a serious political issue, also raise doubts about the survival of self-government in this country. We are embarked on a dangerous trend toward control by a collection of elitists whose interests and inclinations dominate national policy irrespective of the public will, and often at the expense of the public good.

We have no reason to expect popular confidence in government until politicians and public officials begin exhibiting their own confidence in the democratic system and the American people. The electorate has a preeminent right to know what government is doing and why, and to hear the honest judgments of their leaders.

That standard must depend heavily on self-discipline, by candidates and officeholders, and by the press as well. But there are other steps we can take to meet it.

To give the American people the best possible opportunity to evaluate fairly the candidates and the issues in 1972, I propose the following immediate steps:

—All candidates, both in the primaries and in the general elections, should stand ready to participate in public debates.

—All candidates should offer an opportunity for questions from the public on a daily basis.

—All candidates should disclose their personal finances, including sources of income, total assets, and liabilities.

—All candidates should simultaneously disclose lists of campaign contributions and contributors on a regular basis.

To advance the goal of open government, I propose that the new administration—elected next fall—initiate immediately, by executive order where possible, and by proposed legislation where necessary, the following procedures, none of which are presently in effect:

—Regular presidential press conferences will be held at least twice each month. Follow-up questions will be allowed, to assure that answers are complete.

—Members of the Cabinet will have press conferences at least once each month.

—There will be an end to background briefings in which information is supplied on the condition that the source is not disclosed. All such briefings will be for attribution to the official who conducts them.

—Cabinet meetings will be open to the press except in rare cases where national security imposes a secrecy requirement.

—All presidential appointees will be required to disclose assets, income, and liabilities.

—Regular reports will be available on contacts by lobbying organizations and special-interest groups with all officials whose responsibilities affect the formation of national policy.

—The professional personnel responsible for the collection of statistical information under government auspices will be available for press briefings and interviews, without exception.

—The budgets of all federal agencies, including those involved in intelligence work, will be disclosed.

—Classification of documents or classes of documents will be allowed only upon order of the President, the Vice-president, and officials confirmed by the Senate, and a decision to classify must be made within thirty days of production of the document. This process will be open to monitoring by the Congress.

—A systematic procedure for automatic declassification of

documents will be adopted, providing in general that classification may not last longer than two years.

—A unit in the Budget Bureau will report annually on recipients of benefits from federal subsidy programs, including not only direct payments but tax benefits, special mail rates, concessional interest rates, deposits of federal revenues, and other forms of privilege.

—The federal government will encourage the adoption of a uniform open-government statute for the states, including public disclosures of assets, liabilities, and income by high state and local officials; publication of the distribution of the state and local tax burden by income classes; publication of recipients of state and local benefits and subsidies, including direct payments, tax privileges, property valuation discrepancies, and special services.

The Corruption of America

By early October, the issue of corruption had not yet taken hold; indeed, it was not finally to do so until the next spring, months after the election. But I believed that this was the most corrupt administration in American history—and I decided to say so bluntly at the UPI Editors Conference in Washington. The speech was widely criticized at the time. It was dismissed as a desperate tactic—which it was not— or as alarmist hyperbole—when events have proved that it was in fact understated. As I reread it now, I am especially satisfied by its comprehension that the corruption at issue was not just a matter of dirty money but of liberties subverted and ideals perverted. I think the nation now sees more clearly, after Watergate, the "White House horrors," the perversion of campaign financing, the "enemies" list and all the rest, ad nauseam, how pervasive and dangerous the corruption of America had become.

This speech and others do illustrate that at least the outlines of the corruption that has since shocked us so deeply were already apparent in 1972. Its very seriousness may be part of the reason why it did not penetrate during the campaign—understandably, the American people did not want such things to be true about their government. It was easier to accept the denials and to believe the counter-charge that it was all a pack of lies devised by Democrats and spread by a hostile press. Vice-president Agnew's earlier campaign to discredit the media had paved the way. And full comprehension was simply not possible in the heat of a political campaign.

UPI Editors Conference

WASHINGTON, D.C. | OCTOBER 2, 1972

Yesterday on *Meet the Press,* my wife said that the current administration was the most corrupt administration in recent history. I agree with that—with one modification. I would leave out the word "recent."

The corruption of government has come many times in our national experience. In our own time, it has come wearing Sherman Adams' vicuna coat, with Senator Richard Nixon's $18,000 slush fund in the pockets. It was found on the back shelf of General Harry Vaughan's deep freeze. But at no time have we witnessed official corruption as wide or as deep as the mess in Washington right now.

Instead of a vicuna coat buying a letter to a regulatory commission, we hear about a campaign contribution buying a billion-dollar antitrust settlement. Instead of a deep freeze, we hear about a wheat deal that freezes farmers out of their earnings as surely as any frost, while a few grain companies reap fantastic profits. Instead of an $18,000 Nixon slush fund, we hear about a $10 million Nixon secret fund.

And we face not merely the shoddy corruption that permits powerful men to buy what they want from public officials, but the steady corruption of our own precious values as a country. Today, we face not merely the corruption of government but the corruption of America.

The Nixon mess in Washington includes the corruption of our ideals in an unjust war as well as the corruption of the Justice Department in the ITT case. It includes the corruption of our

Constitution by assaults on freedom of the press as well as the corruption of our tax code by loopholes for a wealthy few. It includes the corruption of our political process by attempts to hide the real issues of 1972 as well as the corruption of law enforcement by attempts to hide the truth about the Watergate burglary last June.

The real America is not a corrupt nation.

The real America is a nation whose highest commitment is to the dignity of every living soul. Its essential faith is that each man, woman, and child among us deserves the respect and the protection of government, not because he has wealth or power, not because of his wit or skill or station, but simply because he is a citizen of the United States. Where the pursuit of happiness is the common right of everyone, there cannot be special privileges for anyone.

The real America is a nation born in an abiding distrust of government. Our forebears experienced abuse of power—and they were determined that it would not happen here ever again. So they placed sharp limits on the power of government to wage unwanted wars, to levy unjust taxes, or to carry on the public business without a fair accounting to the people. The quality that made our country unique from the beginning was its insistence that the government must answer to the governed.

And the real America is a nation with such a passion for justice that in the last century it risked its survival in a civil war to secure human freedom—and in this century, when terror and tyranny threatened Europe, it took up arms and laid down lives once more.

Most of all, the real America is a nation bound together by a sense of national purpose, by a sense of confidence that this great experiment shall succeed. The United States exists because a tiny band of rebels were foolish enough—and faithful enough —to take on the mighty arms of an empire. That same spirit explored and settled an unknown continent and healed the wounds of war. It carried our farmers through the dust storms of the 1930's and our workers through the Depression to a New

Deal. It is the quiet patriotism which is determined to build and then endure, and then build anew.

And it is all of this—the enduring values and the proud heritage of two hundred years—that is denied by the corruption of America.

Today, an unjust war corrupts our principles.

Four years ago, the American people were offered peace, and they accepted. Now we know the war could end at any moment, if we would only break free from the brutal regime in Saigon. Yet the promise of peace remains a lie.

Our sacred honor is laid at the feet of dictators, dope-runners and gangsters in Saigon—a government that subverts our ideals just as eagerly as it steals our aid.

And in defense of that government, the most incredible bombardment the world has ever seen now rains down on helpless people in Indochina. While General Thieu is secure in his palace, six million of his South Vietnamese countrymen are victims—dead, maimed, or driven from their homes.

The bombing does not save the South Vietnamese; it destroys them. And while it does that, it corrupts the compassion and the humanity of our people.

The real America stands for peace, against an unjust war.

In 1972, our leaders are also corrupting the Constitution in an effort to hide their failures and hoard their power.

This administration has tried to bully the press into docile submission. It has launched a deliberate, sustained campaign to discredit newspapers and broadcasters. It has misused federal law enforcement officers to investigate the personal lives of reporters. And for the first time in our history, we have seen the government attempt to prevent—and then to punish—the publication of critical facts—not because it harmed the country, but because it embarrassed the government.

This administration seeks to replace a press corps with a cheering section—with a propaganda machine that is in league with the government, to be used by the government, to tell the people what the government wants them to hear.

This administration has tried to destroy the separation of powers. For four years, they have been so intent on making war that they have denied both the responsibility of the Congress to say "yes" and the right of the Congress to say "no." Cambodia was invaded without a glance toward Capitol Hill. And when Senator Mansfield proposed legislation to end the war, Mr. Nixon proudly announced—in advance—that if it were passed, it would be ignored.

Not content with this, the administration has proudly made the worst Supreme Court nominations in American history—and then attacked the Congress for exercising its duty to advise before it consents.

That is how the Constitution stands corrupted after four Nixon years.

The real America stands in respect of the Constitution, against those who would debase the rule of law.

Finally, the politics of evasion today corrupts the political process itself.

Free discussion and the competition of ideas should be at the heart of our system. They were in 1960, when John Kennedy and Richard Nixon met in a series of face-to-face television debates and openly discussed the issues before the American people. Even though most observers agreed that Mr. Nixon lost the election because he lost the debates, he wrote afterwards: ". . . joint TV appearances of candidates at the presidential level are here to stay. . . . The candidates have a responsibility to inform the public of their views before the widest possible audience."

I think that Mr. Nixon was right when he wrote that, but evidently he has changed his mind. Evidently he assumes that he can now evade the issues. He assumes that Americans will not demand answers. He assumes that he can hide at the White House, without explaining his record, defending his conduct, or detailing his plans for the future.

And this may be the most insidious corruption of all—for when a candidate does not level with the country, the people lose their liberty. They are deprived of that fair opportunity to reckon and choose, which alone assures their control over the great decisions of the next four years.

The White House says the President is too busy to debate—but he is not too busy to address three fund-raising luncheons and dinners in twenty-four hours. He is not too busy to spend an evening campaigning among the rich at John Connally's ranch. All we ask is an hour of his time to discuss the great decision of 1972, but Richard Nixon is too busy for the American people.

Vice-president Agnew says that there is no reason for a debate because there are no questions to be answered. In his mind it is perfectly clear that the Republicans deserve another four years. But five million unemployed workers, millions of citizens without special favors from Washington, and the families of our prisoners of war at least have the right to ask, "Four more years of what?"

I suspect that the true reason Richard Nixon will not debate is that he is afraid—not of me, but of the people. He must realize that if he is forced to tell them what he really has in store, there will be little doubt of his defeat in November.

I am not afraid of open debate. I would welcome it. For a candidate cannot lie about his opponent's positions when his opponent is there to correct him. A candidate cannot conceal his plans when his opponent is there to ask questions.

I have read in recent news surveys that I am in trouble with some voters because I have changed my mind on selection of Senator Eagleton as my running mate, and on details of my tax and welfare plans. It is said that these changes suggest uncertainty and undermine my credibility in comparison with a more reliable and competent record by Mr. Nixon.

If that, indeed, is the comparative public perspective of Mr. Nixon and me, it represents one of three failures or perhaps all three: first, a failure by me to communicate my real character and veracity to the voters; second, a masterful political selling job by Mr. Nixon; or third, a possible inability by some of the press to bring the same critical examination to the two candidates. I make no apology for changing my mind in light of additional insight and reflection. Indeed, a leader who is afraid to change his mind for fearing of losing face is no leader at all— he is a disaster, as witness our experience in Vietnam.

I feel especially that I handled the matter of Senator Eagleton's candidacy with compassion and with concern for the best interests of the nation. It is no accident that Senator Eagleton is now campaigning for my election and that his popularity has been enhanced, not diminished. The nation can ill afford to debate this issue while death stalks the face of Indochina and our leadership at home is ineffective and insensitive.

I have never deceived the American people and I have not ducked the hard questions of war and peace, the defense budget, and tax reform. Furthermore, I have held to a steady course on the transcendent issues of our time—the war in Vietnam and the reallocation of excessive military spending to the urgent needs of our society. I see Mr. Nixon in contrast as a man of no constant principle except opportunism and political manipulation. But the voters, hopefully with the help of a diligent, even-handed press, must make the final judgment between Richard Nixon and George McGovern.

So today I am challenging the Republican candidate to meet me and to face the American people openly in public debate. He can choose the format.

It is a corruption of the political process to turn the national election into a guessing game, where the people are asked to elect a president without knowing what he would do if he won.

The real America stands against this politics of stealth and for the right of the people to know before they decide.

Someday this moment that seems so real to us will exist only in memory and in history. How will we look a generation from now?

Will our grandchildren read that these were the years of scandal—and no one cared; that these were the years of lost ideals—and no one cared; that these were the years of the corruption of America—and our answer was not outrage but four more years?

The answer is up to us—all of us—the people, the candidates, and the press.

The people will do their part if they are given the chance. They do not want a government whose symbol is a paper-shredder. They want a government that rights wrongs instead of committing them. They are not left, or right, or center; rather they seek a way out of the wilderness.

It is the responsibility of the candidates to point the way, each according to his own vision. And if a candidate fails this responsibility—if he offers no vision and no plans, if he runs for the most powerful office in America by running away from the issues—then the success or failure of the system depends on the press.

The work of the press is hardest when it is most important.

When a candidate issues press releases but holds no press conferences, it is up to the reporters to inform the country that he is hiding. When a candidate tells lies to a hand-picked crowd, it is up to reporters to tell the country the truth. And when a candidate will not give answers, it is up to the reporters to keep asking questions—or to keep reminding people of what they would ask if the candidate would come within shouting distance.

I am not suggesting that it is right for reporters to take sides. But though the press should never be a partisan of party, it should always remain a partisan of the principle that the people must have all the facts.

I intend to campaign all-out in the last five weeks before Election Day.

I intend to carry the Democratic message to every voter despite Republican distortions and evasions.

And I believe that on November 7, the people will end the corruption of America and restore the real America.

Then our children and their children after them will love America, not just because they were born here, but because of the great and good land you and I together have made it.

Help from Skinny Cats

Whether or not the truism is always right, most of us do perceive that money is the root of much political evil. Its political power tells a whole lot about why the tax system favors the rich; why a huge aerospace corporation gets bailed out while small business firms go broke; why "crime in the suites" is ignored while government agents are busy investigating those who demonstrate against government policy; why, in sum, many Americans have lost faith that government serves them or that democracy works.

I tried to address that concern not only by the nature of my proposals, but by the sources of my financing as well. What better evidence could there be that I was beholden not to special interests who wanted to buy a share of the government, but to ordinary people who wanted to help pay for a better country. So most of the money raised came from small contributions, through direct mail campaigns and five-dollar-a-plate "People's Fund-raisers" like the one in Des Moines on October 6, 1972.

Since then we have moved further toward campaign-financing reform legislation with real teeth—with tough spending ceilings, enforceable limits on individual contributions, and more complete disclosure of who is putting up how much money. Public financing of campaigns has become an attractive alternative to the outrageous big money abuses of 1972. But as we also learned, laws probably never can really control those who believe they can escape law enforcement—those who break the rules to underwrite the winner, knowing he will in turn control the Justice Department. Laws were broken, and, were it not for the special investigative efforts inspired by pervasive corruption, it could be that the violations would never have been uncovered. So regardless of what reforms are adopted, campaign financing will continue to require thorough scrutiny as it is going on—not just after the fact. And candidates must accept a special responsibility for the integrity of everyone who operates on their behalf in this sensitive area.

"People's Dinner"

DES MOINES, IOWA | OCTOBER 6, 1972

I am delighted to be here at this great people's fund-raising dinner.

As I look around this pavilion tonight, I am more convinced than ever that we are going to have a great victory on November 7.

We're going to have a great victory because this year the pollsters and the pundits are wrong, and the people are right.

We're going to have a great victory because we've got the people, and they've got John Connally and his fat-cat friends—and I say that makes the score two for us and none for them.

Now this is called a "people's fund-raiser." You've received a few pieces of chicken and an apple for $5. Unfortunately, there's not much money left over. After four years of Nixon's inflation, a few pieces of chicken and an apple cost almost $5.

But $5 a dinner is still a bargain. When Mr. Nixon finally emerged from the White House last week, he had a few fund-raisers of his own. Only they were $1,000-a-plate dinners. Now if you're asking yourself who would spend that kind of money, it's obvious: Those who want the best government money can buy.

Most of our campaign is being financed by people like you, average people, who have contributed five dollars or ten or twenty because they believe it's time for the people of this country to elect a president for themselves, not for the special interests.

The directors of the Lockheed Corporation have a president. Mr. Nixon makes sure that Lockheed can keep its profits, but the American taxpayer will take care of the losses.

Isn't it time *we* had a president? Isn't it time the small businessmen and farmers who run into financial trouble had a president?

John Connally and his oil-company friends have a president. Mr. Nixon makes sure they keep their oil depletion allowance and their oil import quotas even though they cost the American taxpayer seven billion dollars a year.

Isn't it time *we* had a president? Isn't it time the people who buy the gas and oil in this country had a president?

The executives at ITT have a president. Mr. Nixon makes sure that there are men running the Department of Justice who will drop an important antitrust case against this huge conglomerate just about the same time it agrees to underwrite $400,000 of the cost of the Republican National Convention.

Isn't it time *we* had a president? Isn't it time the people who can't buy off government had a president?

The big grain companies like Continental and Cargill have a president. And they also have a vice-president. His name is Clarence Palmby, and he used to work for us at the United States Department of Agriculture. But he went to work for Continental Grain Company soon after he returned from Moscow where he headed the United States' negotiating team. It was not long before he was back in Washington, talking to the Russian trade officials who one week later made their largest purchase of wheat from Continental. And all of this took place before any announcement of the Russian wheat deal was made to the American people.

Isn't it time *we* had a president? Isn't it time the people who produced all that wheat we are sending to Russia had a president?

When Mr. Nixon submitted Earl Butz's name for confirmation last year, I joined with Harold Hughes and Oren Lee Staley of the N.F.O. and Tony Dechant of the Farmers' Union and most of the farm-state Senators to oppose that nomination.

We examined his career very carefully. It was clear to me then that he was thoroughly committed to the gentlemen farmers in agribusiness, who couldn't tell a chicken coop from a chain store.

For a time, Mr. Butz's popularity increased as the Administration tried to throw its election-year arms around farmers, after turning its back on them for three years.

But the way Mr. Butz and the Department of Agriculture have handled the Russian wheat deal confirms something I suspected all along.

You can take Butz out of the board room, but you can't take the board room out of Butz.

If this administration is so concerned about farmers, why did they quietly telephone the Big Six grain companies and warn them a day ahead of time that the export subsidy was being lowered, but not call one single farm organization?

If this administration is so concerned about farmers, why did they fight against a bill that I supported to compensate the farmers who sold their wheat early because those farmers did not know what the Department of Agriculture and the big grain companies knew?

If the President and the Professor are so concerned about farmers, why did they work to defeat a bill introduced last year by your own Congressman Neil Smith—a bill which I supported—to raise price supports for corn by 25 percent? That defeat at the hands of this administration cost Iowa farmers $240 million.

And if this administration is so concerned about farmers, why won't they back the bill in Congress that Senator Hughes and I support to prohibit giant non-farm conglomerates from taking over family farms?

I'm afraid the answer is obvious: There aren't many farmers on that list of contributors to Mr. Nixon's $10 million secret campaign fund. But I expect there are a fair number of agribusiness executives on the list.

I doubt whether the names of the two million men and women this administration has thrown out of work or the six million people this administration has thrown onto welfare are on that secret list of contributors, either. They can't afford four more years of an economic policy that has meant freedom for big business to raise their profits and prices, and "freedom" for working people to walk the streets and look for a job.

I doubt whether the names of many average housewives are on that list. They can't afford four more years of frozen wages, rising prices, and a shrinking dollar.

I doubt whether the names of many ordinary American taxpayers are on that list. They can't afford four more years of an unfair tax system. There is something fundamentally wrong with a tax system that permits a business executive to deduct the cost of his $20 martini lunch, while a worker cannot deduct the cost of his bologna sandwich.

I expect that it is not the *victims* of the last four years who are on the list of contributors to the secret fund, but the beneficiaries—the corporations who received an $80 billion ten-year tax break from this administration, the companies who have benefited from this administration's relaxation of the antitrust laws, the industries who have been permitted to regulate themselves.

Favoritism toward big business is second nature to this administration. We see it in their "trickle-down" economics, which means you give big business the whole loaf and maybe there will be a few crumbs left over for working people.

And we see it in their double standard of justice—one for their friends and one for the public.

I think the people want some changes made in Washington.

I think the people of this country want an end to the longest, the cruelest, and the stupidest war in our history.

Four years ago next Monday, candidate Richard Nixon said to the American people—and I quote—"Let me make one thing clear. Those who have had a chance for four years and could not produce peace should not be given another chance."

Ladies and gentlemen, I say: For once let's hold Richard Nixon to his word.

I think the American people desperately want an end to this war, and they want it now.

And I think the American people want a government once again that will tell them the truth, even if what is true is not what is popular. When was the last time this president told us something we did not want to hear? If there is so much good news, why aren't things better?

And finally, I believe the American people want a president who will break the stranglehold the special interests have on our government. They want an end to government-for-the-highest-bidder.

So together, let's reclaim our government from the power brokers and their servants in this administration.

Together, let's declare a new Declaration of Independence— independence of government from the privileged few.

And together, let's restore the passion for truth and simple justice to our national leadership.

Give Us Back Our Government

By mid-October, while there were a few contrary signs, we could sense that the corruption issue was simply not getting through. Ben Bagdikian suggested part of the reason for that phenomenon in an article, "The Fruits of Agnewism," in the first post-election issue of *Columbia Journalism Review*. Coverage of the Watergate affair was analyzed closely. And while a few reporters were pursuing it, it was just not being carried around the country. Editors treated the charges with deep skepticism if they were treated at all, while White House responses were given prominent play. So even this late in the campaign, many people probably still thought Watergate was a dam somebody wanted to build, instead of a symbol of political crime.

I concluded that we might be approaching the issue from the wrong slant. Perhaps people could not get excited about one group of politicians spying on other politicians. "Even if it is true," they might wonder, "so what? I can't see how it hurts me." But the Watergate burglary itself was a minor matter. In this speech in Seattle, I described how corruption and big money influenced government policy against the interests of ordinary people. And I made a series of specific pledges and legislative recommendations to guard against abuses of that kind in a McGovern administration. One of

those proposals—for an "Office of Investigations" to supplement the Justice Department in cases involving officials
of the Executive Branch—remained relevant through 1973,
as the country debated whether there should be an independent special prosecutor to investigate political and
official corruption.

King County Bar Association

SEATTLE, WASHINGTON | OCTOBER 13, 1972

I am grateful for your invitation to speak here about a critical
issue in the 1972 campaign.

There is no shortage of sharp policy differences between
President Nixon and me. On the war, on the economy, on taxes,
on crime, on a dozen other issues, we have sharply different
views of the proper course for America. He has described the
campaign as the "choice of the century." And I agree.

But we must be equally concerned—and I think even more
concerned this year—about the environment in which those
policies are made and carried out, and about the influences that
are brought to bear.

Our tradition in this country is that government is the instrument of the people. Our essential faith is that each man, woman,
and child among us deserves the respect and protection of
government, not because he has wealth or power, not because
of his wit or skill or station, but simply because he is a citizen
of the United States.

In America, government derives its power from the people,
and it must provide equal service to them all.

But today those principles have become so corroded that
many Americans have given up in despair.

Government cannot serve two masters.

And I suggest today that government is serving money more

than people. I suggest that the influence of big money has become so pervasive in Washington that the American people are being systematically denied the protection they deserve.

The cumulative power of government is almost beyond imagination. It decides how much of our income we keep and how much is taxed away. It sends our sons to war. It essentially determines how many of us have jobs, what interest rates we pay, whether the laws will be enforced, whether prices will go up or down. It reaches deeply into the daily lives of us all.

Every time that enormous power is abused, a part of democracy dies. And I am alarmed by the growing evidence that the present administration has abused that power as a matter of course.

Consider these examples:

We know that the Department of Justice dropped a major antitrust case against ITT precisely at the time that the company agreed to underwrite $400,000 in Republican convention costs.

Whose interests did that decision represent? Certainly not the American people.

We know that another antitrust action, to block the merger of two giant companies, Parke-Davis and Warner-Lambert, was also dropped by the Justice Department against the strong recommendation of the government's top antitrust lawyer. The honorary chairman of one of those companies is a close friend of Mr. Nixon and a big contributor to his campaigns.

Whose interest did that decision represent? Certainly not the people who pay for high-priced drugs.

We know that the Price Commission wrote a narrow exemption to free Combined Insurance Company of Chicago, and hardly any other companies, from any price controls at all. The Chairman of the Board of that company is W. Clement Stone, a man who gave $1 million to Mr. Nixon's 1968 campaign, and who has already kicked in $500,000 in 1972.

Whose interests did that decision represent? Certainly not the people who buy insurance.

We know that the Republican Treasury Department granted

a Jones Act waiver for the Liberian ship *Sansineas*, so that it could operate in the American coastal trade. That waiver was worth $6 million to $7 million to the men who owned and controlled the ship. In fact, it was owned by a company set up by Peter Flanigan, a top White House assistant to the President. And until 1985, it is chartered to a company whose president is Mr. Nixon's chief West Coast fund-raiser. Fortunately, this decision was overturned by the alertness and action of Senator Joseph Tydings.

We know that several giant grain companies had inside information on the sale of American wheat to the Soviet Union—information which enabled them to rob unsuspecting farmers of the fruit of their labor. We know the Republican Department of Agriculture granted a special grace period for export subsidies, to swell the windfall profits of the grain companies even more.

Whose interests were represented in that sorry affair? Certainly not the farmers who were gouged, nor the consumers who are paying higher prices for bread, and most certainly not the taxpayer, who was forced to contribute to the profits of the wheat traders.

We know that the same Republican Department of Agriculture withheld an increase in milk price supports, until the milk lobbyists came through with $352,000 in donations to the Republican campaign.

Whose interests were represented in that transaction? If the price increase was a just one, it should have been granted without the demand for a political bribe. Certainly not the ordinary American, who expects government to make decisions on the merits, and not on the money.

We know that the Republican Administration tried every shortcut in the book—and a few that were not—to give federal funds to the Penn Central Railroad. We know that while those machinations were going on, top officials of the Republican Transportation Department and the Republican Treasury Department were keeping the biggest investors in the Penn

Central clued in, so they could dump their stock before Penn Central went broke. And the small investors took the loss.

We know, because your own Senator Magnuson has exposed it, that the nation's carpet manufacturers were promised an indefinite postponement of effective safety regulations—after they collected nearly $95,000 for Mr. Nixon's campaign.

Whose interests were represented in that exchange? Certainly not the people's whose lives are endangered by flammable carpets.

We know that the Federal Power Commission has deregulated the price of most natural gas—an action that means about $10 billion in higher profits for the oil companies. One of the major beneficiaries of that action was Penzoil United, whose president is Mr. Nixon's chief Texas fund-raiser. He collected the money that was sent to Mexico to be "laundered" and that ended up in the hands of the Republican burglars who broke into Democratic headquarters at the Watergate.

Whose interests were represented in that case? Certainly not the consumers, who will have to shell out an extra $10 billion.

And there are other cases that elude public view. They are hidden in Mr. Nixon's $10 million secret campaign fund.

Mr. Nixon and his agents insist that the public has no right to know who gave that $10 million—or what the big givers got in return.

But we know something about how it was raised—by Mr. Stans's vigorous solicitations of business executives and by letters such as the one from a West Coast fund-raiser who told potential donors: "I cannot emphasize too strongly that the protection of your stake and my stake is precisely what is at stake here."

When he signed the law requiring disclosure, Mr. Nixon said this:

"By giving the American people full access to the facts of political campaigning, this legislation will guard against campaign abuses and will work to build public confidence in the integrity of the electoral process."

In light of the record, I frankly don't feel much confidence when I know that Mr. Nixon is sitting on a $10 million secret fund.

How does the Nixon Administration respond?

They begin with a shocking assertion that this is the normal course of events in Washington.

But lesser scandals have rocked the nation.

In 1952, General Eisenhower ordered Richard Nixon to come clean with the American people if he wanted to stay on the Republican ticket—all over an $18,000 fund.

When Mr. Eisenhower was president, his top adviser, Sherman Adams, was fired over a vicuna coat, and the donor went to jail.

Yet today, when we find political money and special favors flowing like Niagara, even the fishiest denials are accepted as explanations. We see a few timid questions, a few artful dodges, and then icy, indifferent silence. And what must the American people think about their government?

Meanwhile, Mr. Nixon staunchly denies responsibility for the whole mess. He refuses to hold press conferences; he refuses to answer questions; he hides in the White House and seeks exoneration in silence.

But the American people know who appointed Earl Butz as Secretary of Agriculture. It was Richard Nixon.

The American people know who appointed and then promoted Richard Kleindienst. The same Richard Nixon.

The American people know who Peter Flanigan works for. And they certainly know who was Murray Chotiner's boss when he milked the dairy industry.

Are we expected to believe that Mr. Nixon does not know what his own staff, and his own Cabinet officers, are up to?

Does anyone think Maurice Stans is just an enthusiastic volunteer, who gathers big gifts on his own? Does anyone believe that Mr. Stans would still refuse to disclose that secret $10 million fund, if he got orders from the White House to do so?

President Truman had a sign in the White House which read, "The buck stops here."

I suggest today that while the dollars may all be flowing to Mr. Stans, the buck still stops in the White House.

We have an urgent task ahead—to break the dangerous link between those in power who seek money, and those with money who seek favors. We must restore the faith of all Americans in a government that will serve the public interest over the special interest.

It will take more than a new administration to restore that faith. We will need new rules, new standards, and new tools.

Toward that end, I am today proposing an Ethics in Government program designed to end present abuses, and to restore the integrity of our government in the eyes of the people.

First, we must sever the link between political contributions and governmental actions. As president, I will urge the Congress to enact the bill I introduced last year to assure all candidates for federal office in the general elections and the primaries a federally financed campaign fund. For the cost of 93 cents for every voter per year, we could provide each major party presidential candidate with $18 million dollars for his campaign, and a similarly adequate fund for candidates for Congress. At the same time, we should set a strict limitation on private political contributions of $50 per person.

Second, as president, I will not allow any special-interest group to plead its case in secret meetings at the White House unless the fact of the meeting and the presentation are made public.

Third, I will urge Congress to enact legislation requiring prior public notice and public transcripts of all ex parte meetings held by regulatory agencies and the departments and agencies under the president's supervision.

Fourth, I will instruct the White House staff to keep hands off the independent regulatory agencies. I will order them not to make any ex parte contact during the pendency of a proceeding—and if they do, I will ask them to resign.

And I will ask the chairman of each regulatory agency, including the Wage Board and the Price Commission, to notify the president and the press of every call or contact from the White House on any adjudicative case before his body. I will remind them that they serve as judges as well as administrators, and that billions of dollars of the taxpayers' money depends on their decisions.

Fifth, I will urge the Congress to strengthen the present laws on conflicts of interest to require a wait of five years before any government employee can take a job with a company with which he has had dealings on behalf of the government.

Sixth, I will urge the enactment of legislation to require full public disclosure of the income, assets and liabilities of every employee of the government whose income exceeds $15,000 a year.

Seventh, I will propose creation of a separate Office of Investigations, to supplement the Department of Justice, with the power to look into charges of illegal activity made against members of the Executive Department or the White House staff. The attorney general is the president's lawyer, and his department cannot act as both prosecution and defense in the same case.

This agency would be independent of both the president and the Congress, and have at its disposal the resources of the Federal Bureau of Investigation.

I believe these reforms would go a long way toward restoring public confidence in the government of the United States. But in the last analysis honesty and ethics in government come down to the attitude of public men themselves. If they take their jobs with an eye toward enhancing their future in private life, no list of rules can keep them from temptation. If, on the other hand, they resolve to guide themselves by the motto that a public office is a public trust, no amount of temptation can keep them from the honest performance of their job.

Those who hold public office for money or for power have had their day in America. The time has come for those who want to serve. Let us dedicate ourselves to restoring for this country the atmosphere of probity in the White House and throughout the government of the United States. Only then can we restore the most precious asset any government can have—the people's firm faith that it is working each day and each hour in their behalf.

It was Franklin D. Roosevelt who said: "The Presidency is above all a place of moral leadership." That is the kind of presidency I want for the people of America.

The Way to Integrity

Our final appeal on the corruption issue was a television address in which I tried to climb directly over the wall of relative news silence on the subject. It pulled together themes I had been developing in rally speeches throughout the summer and fall, and cited case histories documented by my research staff from news accounts and public records. By then political espionage and sabotage—the exploits of Donald Segretti and company—had begun to surface, and I also described the impact of activities of that kind on our free democratic institutions.

I tried to be attentive, too, to the danger of a campaign that appears entirely negative and carping. Part of the answer to that had been to propose specific reforms designed to end the abuses I was describing. But beyond that, I thought it was important to express my essential optimism and faith about America and its people. The country was not corrupt and the system had not failed; rather, a few Americans had failed the system and disgraced themselves. After the campaign and defeat, and after everything else we learned too late for the campaign, I still believe that.

Television Address

OCTOBER 25, 1972

OPENING NARRATION:

Tonight, from the Senate Wing of the Capitol, the candidate of the Democratic Party for the presidency of the United States, George McGovern, speaks to the nation.

SENATOR MCGOVERN:

In earlier broadcasts, I have discussed the choices facing the American people on two critical issues—the war in Vietnam and the economy of America.

Tonight, I ask you to consider another issue that troubles the very soul of our country. The issue is integrity. For although we are concerned about our immediate needs, there is a deeper crisis in America—a crisis of the spirit.

As I have listened to the American people and tried to sense what was in their hearts, one message has come through consistently. It is that people are losing confidence in their leaders.

I saw that in the eyes of an elderly woman in Wisconsin, who told me she feels abandoned by her country.

I heard it in the angry voices of men and women on the assembly lines in Detroit, who asked me why so much of their wages go for taxes when some big interests pay no taxes at all.

I heard it from a badly wounded young Marine in Vietnam last year, who told me: "I will never trust the government again." Too many people have told me: "All politicians are crooked."

When I hear that, I fear for the American future. For our free system of government is founded on trust between those who elect and those who are elected. And when that bond weakens, a part of democracy dies.

Restoring that bond of trust may be the greatest challenge facing the next president of the United States.

A few weeks ago, I suggested to the students at Wheaton College in Illinois that the president of the United States has a responsibility greater than running the government. He must also serve as the moral leader of the nation. He can lift the moral vision of America and rekindle our sense of national purpose.

The present administration is failing that responsibility.

Consider, for example, the enforcement of our antitrust laws. They were written to protect consumers against too much economic power in too few hands. And they safeguard our free-enterprise system, preserving independent business against excessive concentrations of power.

By swallowing up other companies, ITT has become one of the most powerful conglomerates in the country. When ITT wanted to take over still another corporation—one of the nation's largest insurance companies—the Antitrust Division of the Justice Department said that was too much. So they prepared to go into court to stop that merger.

But while the case was being prepared, ITT offered several hundred thousand dollars to finance the Republican National Convention. And what happened then? The antitrust case against ITT was dropped and the company destroyed the evidence of collusion in a shredding machine. Abandonment of that case meant a billon-dollar settlement for ITT, higher costs for you, and less freedom in our free-enterprise system.

When Mr. Nixon decided to abandon his first economic policy because it was not working, he set up a commission that he promised would control the cost of living.

But the Combined Insurance Company of Chicago is not covered. The chairman of that company gave half a million dollars to Mr. Nixon's 1968 campaign, and he has said he plans to give a million dollars this year. Seven days after he had dinner at the White House, the Price Commission gave his company a special exemption from price controls.

Last year, dairy lobbyists were pressing hard for higher milk prices. The Secretary of Agriculture turned them down. But then a long-time adviser of Mr. Nixon met in the White House with the dairy lobbyists. They contributed $352,000 to Mr.

Nixon's campaign. And within a few days, the Secretary of Agriculture reversed his decision and decreed higher prices for milk.

In 1970, thirty-eight older Americans in Ohio lost their lives in a nursing home fire. After careful investigation, authorities traced the cause of that disaster to a highly flammable carpet. The fire became a raging inferno before the people inside even had a chance to be saved. So stronger carpet safety regulations were proposed, to see that nothing like that would ever happen again.

But there was another meeting in the White House—between executives of the carpet industry and top officials of the Republican campaign. They gave almost $95,000 for Mr. Nixon's reelection. And the carpet safety regulations were postponed.

These actions do not demonstrate the moral standards that I believe America wants and expects. What they represent is the immoral influence of big money on the public business.

Last year, the Congress decided to do something about that. We adopted a new law that says you have a right to know where the campaign money is coming from so you can judge whether special favors are involved. We followed the advice of Justice Louis Brandeis: "Sunlight is the best of disinfectants."

Although that disclosure law did not go into effect until April of 1972, my campaign has revealed the name of every contributor since I first became a candidate in January of 1971.

But Mr. Nixon did just the opposite.

Before the disclosure law went into effect, he launched a massive drive to beat the system and to defeat your right to know. By the time of the disclosure deadline, he had collected at least $10 million from powerful supporters.

He has not revealed the name of a single contributor. And that is the secret $10 million fund you have heard about. Mr. Nixon is saying, in effect, that it's none of your business who is bankrolling his campaign.

You have a right to ask candidate Nixon: "Why are you afraid to name your contributors?

If we knew the names on that secret list, we might have the answers to some other troubling questions about why our government has acted the way it has over the past four years.

Why is it that when there is a tax break, it always goes to those who need it least, and never to you?

Why is it that the inefficient managers of Lockheed got bailed out by a government loan, but nothing is done to save the thousands of small businessmen and family farmers who are going broke every year?

Why did this administration help the big grain exporters take advantage of the family farmers on the Russian wheat deal?

And why is it that this administration puts a lid on wages, but lets prices rise on everything you buy?

These are some of the most important decisions our government has made in the last four years. Each time, the special interests won and you lost.

Is it any wonder that confidence in the moral integrity of government is declining?

Mr. Nixon and I disagree on the proper relationship between money, power, and people.

We disagree, as well, on the conduct of political campaigns.

Four months ago, five men wearing rubber gloves and carrying burglar's tools were arrested by the police inside the Democratic Party Headquarters in Washington. They were there in the middle of the night to remove listening devices they had previously planted on the telephones. And they were there to steal private files on Democratic senators, congressmen, and party officials. One of them had $114,000 in his bank account —money that came from the Nixon campaign fund.

And the Democratic headquarters was not their only target.

We now know that these men were part of a nationwide network of at least fifty agents hired by the Nixon campaign to create confusion and division among the Democratic candidates for president. Part of their job was to distort your impressions of those candidates—what kind of men they were, and what they stood for.

You may recall the incident in Manchester, New Hampshire,

in this year's first primary, when Senator Muskie showed his outrage at the unfair things that were printed about him in that city's newspaper. Many people believe that event had a decisive impact on Senator Muskie's chance for the nomination.

The whole affair started with a letter, supposedly from a voter in Florida, accusing Senator Muskie of using insulting language. But that Florida voter was never found. And now we know why. The letter was a forgery. And it has been traced to a White House aide.

This same army of Republican sabotage agents released false statements to the press in the name of Democratic candidates. They tried to place listening devices in my campaign office. They attempted to throw campaign schedules into disarray. They forged letters. They followed our families. They even plotted a disruption of their own Republican convention in Miami Beach so they could blame it on the Democrats.

And all of this was paid for out of a secret $700,000 espionage fund kept in the safe of Mr. Nixon's finance chairman and controlled by John Mitchell, even while he was still attorney general of the United States.

Not one of these facts has been refuted or explained. The only response has been to attack the reporters who searched out the truth.

During eighteen years in politics, I have never seen such efforts to poison the political dialogue. These Republican politicians have fouled the political atmosphere for all of us who see public service as a high calling.

They do not seek to defeat the Democratic Party; they seek to destroy it.

And in the process, they would deny one of the most precious freedoms of all—your freedom to judge which candidate will better serve your interests and truly reflect your view of America.

If our free system is to survive, we must recall that just as you set standards of decency and fair dealing in your own lives, there are accepted limits on what is right in a political contest.

But on the few occasions when they even acknowledge these

actions, Administration officials use terms like "caper" and "prank." They want you to believe that all presidential candidates accept contributions with strings attached. They want you to believe that all politicians wiretap and sabotage and spy, and they always have. That is simply not true.

Special favors and secret funds cannot be ignored.

The crime of burglary cannot be excused by calling it a "caper."

And $700,000 worth of political espionage is no "prank."

The men who have collected millions in secret money, who have passed out special favors, who have ordered political sabotage, who have invaded our offices in the dead of night— all of these men work for Mr. Nixon. Most of them he hired himself. And their power comes from him alone. They act on his behalf, and they all accept his orders.

Yet Mr. Nixon has even promoted some of the officials implicated in the scandals.

And he has blocked any independent investigation. He refuses to answer questions from either the press or the people. He stays hidden in the White House, hoping you will mistake silence for innocence.

In 1961, when the Bay of Pigs invasion turned into disaster, President Kennedy did not duck the issue. He accepted full responsibility for everything that went wrong.

When Harry Truman sat in the White House, he had a sign on his desk: "The buck stops here."

That is the kind of men they were. And that is the kind of responsible presidential leadership we must restore.

Our present leadership has not only failed that test, it has undermined the personal freedom of Americans and the constitutional framework of our government.

We have seen a demeaning of our judicial system with Supreme Court nominations that shocked the nation. Two of those appointments were rejected by the Senate. Two others were stopped short by the American Bar Association. But four of Mr. Nixon's appointments now sit on the Supreme Court. And another four years could easily permit him to dominate the entire court for the rest of this century.

Likewise, the Congress has been undermined by the encroachment of arbitrary executive power. American forces were committed across the Cambodian frontier without so much as a telephone call to leaders of the Congress. Mr. Nixon said of Senator Mansfield's resolution calling for an end to the war that the Administration would ignore any such expression by the Congress. Secret arrangements have been negotiated with foreign powers without the consent or even the knowledge of the Senate Foreign Relations Committee. The warmaking power which the founding fathers lodged in the Congress has been preempted by the Chief Executive. And this abuse of power was made all the more dangerous when a military commander went unpunished even after he conducted bombing raids without the approval of civilian authority.

Other dangerous new practices, such as preventive detention, no-knock searches of our homes, and a requirement that telephone companies and landlords must assist in planting eavesdropping devices—all of these are unprecedented threats to our personal freedoms.

We want to think that our Department of Justice applies the law with an even hand. But conspiracy laws were used to prosecute nuns and priests involved in a war protest, whereas no action was taken when students were killed at Kent State or Jackson State.

We are confronted, in short, with both a moral and a constitutional crisis of unprecedented dimensions. Ambitious men come and go, but a free society might never recover from a sustained assault on its most basic institutions. And one can only ask, If this has happened in four years, to what lengths would the same leadership go in another four years, once freed of the restraints of facing the people for reelection?

The next president will inherit this crisis and this legacy of distrust that has been accumulating over the last four years. It will take time to convince people that they can believe in their government once again. It is not easy to teach respect for law and order when the government itself has scorned the moral and constitutional foundation of law and order.

But it can be done. I believe that a president who keeps faith with the American people will, in time, revive that confidence.

The next president can summon the American people to a higher standard—but only if he sets a higher standard for himself.

He can persuade Americans to care about their fellow human beings—but only if he cares himself.

And the next president can rekindle our love of freedom—but only if he loves freedom more than power.

The next president must understand that freedom is not indestructible. He must heed the warning of Benjamin Franklin, as he stepped out of Independence Hall on the day that America was born.

"What kind of government is it?" someone asked.

"A republic," he said, "if you can keep it."

Benjamin Franklin and the others present in Philadelphia that day had risked their lives to secure their liberty from an oppressive government. They were not about to hand it over to more oppression.

They understand what we must remember—that freedom lost is seldom restored.

And like those early patriots, we must stand as watchmen, guarding our liberty from the advance of overreaching political power, just as we would defend it from an advancing foreign army.

I believe we will keep our republic. We will save the ideals we have cherished for nearly two hundred years.

I believe that because I have been out among the people campaigning.

And this is what I have learned.

The people are not left or right or center. Rather, they seek a way out of the wilderness.

They want a president who will restore their trust in government by trusting them—a leader who will neither distort the truth, nor loan away the government.

They ask for a president who will tell them, not just what they want to hear, but what they have a right to know.

They want a leadership that will return a basic sense of fairness to government—that will set not one standard for the powerful and one for those without power, but a single standard for us all.

They hunger for that clarifying vision of national purpose that only a president can provide—a president who will lift our eyes above the daily entanglements to a more distant horizon, to the time when, as Thomas Paine said, "No land on earth shall be as happy as America."

That is the kind of president I want to be.

A president who will ask the best of our people, so we can glow with a new love for America—and America can lift a new light before the world.

Then our children and their children after them will love this land, not merely because they were born here, but because of the great and good country that you and I together have made it.

Thank you and good night.

A New Definition
of National Security

The most comprehensive position paper of the campaign was an alternative national military posture which called for a very logical but nonetheless very new approach to arms spending.

I had been involved in debates over the military budget almost every year since I came to the Senate in 1963. And the most striking feature of those debates and the votes that followed was the routine manner in which we ratified Pentagon demands for more and more money. We might spend weeks exploring every facet of a $100 million poverty program. But a military budget seven hundred times that size would whisk through with hardly a whimper of dissent. And frequently the justifications for more Pentagon money had very little to do with legitimate military needs.

I proposed a "zero-based" approach in which we would examine the threat we might have to face, account for existing forces, and then build whatever additions were necessary to meet the threat. My alternative budget then spelled out what level of arms spending would be adequate if we proceeded on that basis.

In late May, Secretary of Defense Melvin Laird sharply attacked my proposal in testimony before the Joint Economic Committee. The chairman, Senator Proxmire, invited me to respond, and I welcomed the chance.

Subcommittee on Priorities and Economy in Government, Joint Economic Committee

JUNE 16, 1972

Mr. Chairman and members of the Subcommittee, I am grateful for the opportunity to join in your effort to evaluate national priorities and to look ahead over the next five years.

Your invitation asked that I discuss the alternative military budget, involving a phasedown to $54.8 billion in arms spending by fiscal 1973, which I proposed in January.

There is no more important subject to be considered in hearings of this kind. The truth is that we will have no new national priorities unless we make some dramatic changes in today's military spending trends. And unless we do that, the goal of full employment will remain an empty political pipe dream.

With the Committee's permission I would like to proceed in three steps: first, by describing briefly the size and the meaning of my alternative military budget; second, by outlining some of the thinking behind it; and third, by suggesting its potential impact on the economy and national priorities.

First let me say that I have not proposed cuts in the Nixon Administration's defense budget. I have outlined a military posture for fiscal 1975, and there is no way of knowing what the Nixon Administration, if it were in office, would propose to spend in that year. Instead, my proposal draws on existing forces and makes additions where necessary, to come up with the kind of military force I believe we will need in 1975.

We have estimated the total cost of that program at $54.8 billion. I have seen the analysis by the Assistant Secretary of Defense which disputes that figure, and I can understand his confusion. The tables and labeling at the end of the original paper were misleading. If he had looked beyond the tables and attempted to price out the various elements of the program, I think he would have come up with roughly the same figures we did.

I am not anxious to get in a pricing argument with anyone,

because the focus of our debate obviously ought to be centered on whether the proposed force levels are adequate. But I have attached a complete description of the alternative program, along with a more detailed projection of its costs, at the end of my statement.

My proposal does not require major revisions in American commitments, or a major scaling down in real American security interests. Instead, it changes the manner in which those interests are served, and moves on more practical assessments of when and where U.S. forces might be involved in combat.

The budget retains a firm commitment to nuclear deterrence, and provides abundant power by retaining the triad—bombers, land-based missiles, and missile-firing submarines—and by maintaining substantially more forces than necessary for assured destruction of the potential enemy.

It would keep all the Minuteman missiles and all the Polaris/Poseidon missiles we presently have, including the conversions completed by January of next year. In addition, it would keep two hundred strategic bombers, made up of the later-series B-52's plus four squadrons of FB-111's. Total force loadings would be well in excess of those of the Soviet Union, and more than ten times the number required to destroy every significant target in both the Soviet Union and the People's Republic of China.

Aside from negotiating tactics, the major new assumption is that the triad should be seen as a vehicle for stability rather than military excess. It should permit us to wait longer before moving ahead with new deployments, by assuring that our deterrent will remain secure even though there might be a temporary risk to one or another of its elements.

The proposals also call for reductions in strategic air defense, on the premise that since no defense against missile attack is possible—in fact such a defense is now prohibited—it is irrelevant to build a defense against the limited Soviet bomber fleet.

The U.S. commitment to NATO, our highest priority overseas defense commitment, would be fully met.

The proposal calls for eight divisions of active land forces in NATO, which fulfills the apportioned share of the United States. It programs sixteen tactical airwings for Europe, or two more than the U.S. share.

However, two and one-third of the four and one-third divisions now stationed in Europe would be gradually returned to the United States, after full consultation with our European allies. Two land divisions would remain, and six in the United States would be available for rapid redeployment, using new airlift capacity, in case of heightened tensions or build-ups on the Warsaw Pact side.

The firm U.S. commitment to the survival of Israel would be maintained, and there would be no lessening of the demonstrated U.S. interest in the Middle East.

The most critical military need in the Middle East is to assist Israel in maintaining the balance of forces, by providing modern aircraft and other military supplies so the Israelis themselves can deter further aggression. At the same time, the alternative budget contemplates two carrier task forces in or within range of the Mediterranean, to demonstrate our firm commitment to Israel and our determination to see an ultimate settlement which provides secure and recognized boundaries.

The proposal is based on the conclusion that the prospect for further direct U.S. military involvement in Asia is extremely remote.

The first priority in Asia would be to end our involvement in Indochina just as quickly as that can be accomplished. I am convinced that all U.S. troops could be brought out, and all U.S. prisoners of war and missing in action would be released or accounted for, within ninety days of a decision to pursue those goals.

A more literal reading of the one and one-half war planning assumption would permit further reductions in U.S. forces stationed in or oriented toward Asia, on the theory that we need not plan for a major war in Europe and in Asia at the same time. But regardless of what general planning assumption is used, it is realistic to doubt very strongly the premise that American forces might be called upon to confront Chinese forces in Asia. The People's Republic of China has formidable defensive forces, but hardly any standing capacity to wage conventional war outside her own borders. And the Chinese army is heavily preoccupied along an extensive common border with the Soviet Union.

Elsewhere in Asia noncommunist governments have formidable defensive capabilities of their own. South Korea has numerical superiority over the North, and the effect of recalling the remaining U.S. division in Korea would be offset by the return of Korean forces now fighting in Vietnam.

But while the alternative budget does not signal a lessened American commitment to our real security interests, it does pose a firm challenge to practices and tactics which have driven military costs sharply upward and which have frustrated attempts to control arms spending.

It is a zero-based budget, set by evaluating the threats which must be faced rather than by comparison with spending in the past.

Military spending decisions are almost always measured according to how much we have been spending, or how much we spent last year. Yet such descriptions lead to seriously distorted perceptions of our military posture. Where new weapons are concerned, for example, a decision to forgo new spending is usually called a "cut," "unilateral disarmament," or something worse. In fact, it is nothing of the kind. Turning down a new weapon does not reduce the existing force at all. If we spend $20 billion on new weapons in one year and $5 billion the next, we have not cut our military force. We have increased it by $5 billion.

The year-to-year budgetary practice leads to outrageous influences on defense spending. The Budget Bureau frequently sets the final total submitted to the Congress on the basis of whether or not we want to impress the Russians that year, irrespective of what the money is spent for or whether our forces in the field are fully sufficient already to impress the Russians.

I propose a return to reality and common sense in military budgeting. We should examine the physical threats which we and our allies must face in the foreseeable future. Then we should determine the strategic and conventional force levels needed to meet those threats, drawing on existing forces—including those of our allies—and building additions where they are necessary. No part of the current budget should be deemed sacrosanct simply because it exists; instead we should start from "zero" and then retain and construct the forces which can be honestly related to realistic defense needs.

That process would be greatly assisted by projections of national spending patterns—for both military and civilian programs—several years into the future. My alternative military budget is based on a three-year projection, but we can project further than that. Obviously changed conditions would mean changes in actual spending. But advance targets would help the Pentagon to make its plans, the Congress to set national priorities, and the public to understand how well all of us are fulfilling our responsibilities.

The alternative budget also challenges current notions about the kinds of forces which will be useful in the modern context—it rejects inertia in military planning.

Some of the greatest pressures for higher defense spending come from romantic attachments to old systems and strategies which have become obsolete.

I frankly think, for example, that it is extremely dangerous to rely on aircraft carriers in any potential confrontation with the Soviet Union. They could be put out of commission—if not sunk—within a very short time after the war started.

Yet war at sea with the Soviet Union provides the justification for maintaining and modernizing most of the current carrier force and escorts, plus the procurement of carrier-based anti-submarine aircraft, plus the F-14, plus the Phoenix missile.

Both our pocketbook and our security would be far better

served if we simply recognized and accepted the limitations of
aircraft carriers, retained them for functions which they can be
expected to perform, and then concentrated on more realistic
strategies to meet the threat as it evolves.

In short, I think our military planners should be looking to
the future, instead of spending their time trying to justify, and
the taxpayer's money trying to protect, traditional approaches
which can be followed now only at enormous cost and, even
then, can make only a marginal contribution.

My proposal also differs sharply with the "bargaining chip"
theory of negotiations, as practiced by the Nixon Administration.

I welcome and applaud the agreements which have come out
of the Strategic Arms Limitation Talks—particularly the limitation on ABM's.

But at the same time I think it's fair to say that the "bargaining chip" strategy—under which we began building our own
ABM's and MIRV's long before there was any military necessity—has been exposed as a grave and costly tactical blunder.
And it is one the Administration seems determined to repeat.

Tugging the MIRV cat out of the bag has seriously com-
pounded the problems of inspection. So we have ended up with
a limited arms control agreement which completely leaves out
the qualitative jumps that have become the real arms race issue
in recent years.

By exercising restraint, I believe we could have prevented
both Soviet and American MIRV's. But because we were so
determined to play them, we have lost those "bargaining chips."
And now the Administration is back before the Congress demanding more.

Certainly our ability to build these systems should be just as
effective for bargaining purposes as actual construction. My
approach would be similar to that followed by Presidents Eisenhower and Kennedy in achieving the nuclear test ban treaty—
to buy and build weapons solely according to military necessity,
and to hold fast against actions which can only push up the
terms of ultimate arms control agreements. That means that

instead of accelerating the ULMS and B-1 programs now, we should be back at SALT immediately seeking a mutual freeze on further deployments.

At the same time, the alternate budget proposes major reforms in military manpower and procurement practices.

The Brookings Institution's study, "Setting National Priorities —the 1973 Budget," has projected that the next generation of tactical aircraft could cost $40 to $50 million for each plane if costs continue growing at the same rate as they have in the past. The same incredible cost escalation has been occurring virtually across the board.

Aside from plain contractor and procurement sloppiness, one big reason has been the pressure to buy the latest and most exotic military technology, whether or not it provides a significant marginal improvement. That trend means that if there are to be any overall arms budget constraints at all, we will end up with sharply reduced combat capabilities, particularly since performance usually does not live up to paper expectations.

The problem is aggravated by the fact that we usually have only one option. The services develop their dream machines and then offer them to the Office of Management and Budget and to the Congress on a "take it or leave it" basis. A further upward pressure on costs has been the tendency to build too many capabilities—some of them inconsistent—into the same vehicle.

The Senate Armed Services Committee has suggested some fiscal discipline in one case, by choosing the AX over the Cheyenne and the Harrier for close air support. There are alternatives for the Navy F-14, the Air Force F-15, and for other systems as well. What I am proposing is that we move toward simpler designs and more specialized systems, and that we postpone technical innovations until they can have a truly significant impact on overall capabilities.

By far the biggest single increase in military costs in recent years has been in the area of military manpower. Pay raises have been necessary to allow recruitment of an all-volunteer force and to achieve comparability with civilian pay. But those same increases provide strong motive for assuring that our manpower is used effectively.

At the present time, our military establishment is ridiculously top-heavy. We have 5,000 more officers above the equivalent rank of lieutenant colonel—colonels, generals, commanders, captains, and admirals—than we had in 1964, to command about 190,000 fewer men. Returning to the grade distribution pattern of 1964, still heavily weighted in the upper ranks, would save about $1.3 billion in pay and related costs for the same sized force, and substantially more for the force level I have proposed.

The transition to a voluntary force should permit further manpower reductions in such areas as training, rotation, and the ratio of support to combat forces.

I think this country must grasp a broader definition of national security.

Certainly we must address the external threats to our own survival and to our vital interests around the world. My alternative defense proposal does that, and I stand by it. It provides all the forces we need for our own protection, and roughly again as much to assist in the defense of other nations.

But the American people are concerned with other kinds of security as well.

The plain truth is that the major danger to American society today is not threats from abroad but the deterioration of our society from within. We have been so obsessed with the fear of "international Communism" and have spent so much of our energy and resources to feed that fear, that we have robbed and weakened our domestic society. America can now best serve its own interests and the world community by devoting less of our resources to concerns overseas and investing more in the building of our own nation.

President Eisenhower warned in 1953:

• "Every gun that is made, every warship launched, every rocket fired, signifies, in the final sense, a theft from those who hunger and are not fed, those who are cold and are not clothed.

• "The world in arms is not spending money alone. It is spending the sweat of its laborers, the genius of its scientists, and the hopes of its children. . . .

• "This is not a way of life at all, in any true sense. Under the cloud of threatening war, it is humanity hanging from a cross of iron."

Those words ring with devastating truth today.

This subcommittee has heard the budget and deficit projections in recent weeks. You know that the Administration has so far accumulated more than $90 billion in red ink—that about one-fifth of our total national debt has been piled up since Mr. Nixon took office. And you know that military obligations to be incurred this year will grow to a minimum of $85 billion by 1975, even if we leave out new weapons we know nothing about and even if we neglect the cost escalation which has become an absolute certainty in military spending. The Brookings Institution has projected an arms budget of $100 billion by 1977 in current dollars.

So you are fully aware, as I am, that plans for new action on domestic priorities, whether they come from the president, from the Congress, or from presidential candidates, will amount to empty phrases unless we find new sources of funding. If we do not transfer funds from war to peace priorities, there will be no new peace priorities at all.

We are paying the trade-offs now.

In California, there are schools in such a bad state of repair that they will collapse in the next earthquake.

Try telling those children that North Vietnamese guerrillas threaten them more than a schoolhouse that might come crashing down on their heads.

In South Dakota, we do not have enough doctors and nurses and we lack the basic emergency medical services that could use existing technology to save lives. Such conditions are repeated throughout the country, especially in rural areas and central cities.

I think we can make a greater contribution to our security by meeting those needs, instead of feeding the Air Force preference for an elaborate F-15 aircraft, over a simpler version that could perform the major missions better.

New York City loses more lives from drug addiction each year than the whole state of New York lost in Vietnam, at the peak of the fighting. Well over half of all the crime in that city is related to drugs.

I think effective action to crack down on drug pushers, and to find and rehabilitate drug addicts, will make far more difference to the security of New Yorkers than a gold-plated new bomber.

For most Americans our system of transportation is a disgrace. Our air is fouled by deadly exhaust gases, and mass transit—where it exists—is unclean, uncomfortable, and unsafe.

I think building decent public transportation systems will influence our security far more than the effort to hang on to obsolete aircraft carrier strategies.

The Administration wants to turn back $1 billion in food program funds—to retreat further on our commitment to make sure that no American lacks basic nutrition.

I think that issue has more to do with our security than keeping 5,000 superfluous top officers in our armed forces.

These are some of the security choices we have to face.

What I suggest to the committee is that the most serious national security questions today involve such issues as the health of our people, the quality of our schools, the safety of our streets, the condition of our environment, and the vitality of our economy.

The issue is clearly defined between those needs and more arms. And we can postpone it no longer.

I contend as well that we must break our dependence on arms spending in order to achieve full employment.

We are familiar with the priorities costs and the security dangers of excessive arms spending. But we have paid too little attention to the economic consequences—to the fact that mili-

tary spending is among the least efficient methods of creating
and maintaining employment.

I propose to make a direct and immediate shift of arms
dollars to urgent civilian needs. Economists working with me
have developed a projection of what the employment effects of
this exchange would be, assuming a transfer of $32 billion over
a four-year period.

They have concluded that at the end of four years we would
have created at least five million jobs in the civilian sector, replacing all the jobs lost in the armed forces and military industries and adding about 1.5 million new jobs besides. Stated
another way, every $1 billion transferred to new priorities would
create a net increase of 39,000 jobs the first year, 45,000 in the
second, 47,000 in the third, and 48,000 in the fourth.

To deal with acute unemployment problems right now, we
should precede that phased transfer with an immediate $10
billion investment in job-creating enterprises, principally in
housing, transportation, environmental protection, and public
service employment. If adopted immediately, an investment of
that kind would reduce the unemployment rate to no more than
4.3 percent by the middle of next year.

In sum, if we reduce our dependence on arms spending, if
we abandon the bad habit of trying to stimulate the economy by
running more funds through corporate treasuries in special tax
breaks, and if we begin investing directly in urgent public priorities, then full employment can become not a perpetually
frustrated prospect but a realistic hope in the next several years.
With these steps, we can guarantee a job for every man and
woman who wants to work.

In addition, special steps are needed to account for transitional
dislocations during the shift from war to peace priorities.

It is plainly unjust to expect a small minority of Americans—
workers in arms and aerospace industries—to carry by themselves the whole cost of achieving new national priorities.

A phased transfer of the kind I have proposed, coupled with

steps to stimulate the civilian economy and to give arms contractors long-range notice on national spending plans, would mean that long-term unemployment would not be a threat to anyone. As old arms contracts are phased out we will be providing new contracts in the civilian sector to replace them. The companies involved will have fully adequate notice to gear up for peacetime production.

In the interim period, I think we have an obligation to provide income support to the individuals who do lose their jobs, both to protect against personal hardship and to prevent sharp economic dislocations in the communities which have become most heavily dependent on military contracts.

In addition, we should adopt a strong commitment to peacetime scientific and technical priorities, to deal with the special problems facing aerospace scientists and engineers. Legislation currently pending in the Congress, S. 32, sponsored by Senator Kennedy, would have a great impact in assuring that our scientific and technical talents can be put to work quickly on accumulated human needs.

The Economy of Peace

Our aim was more than to reduce wasteful military spending; it was also to redirect useful technological and human resources to truly important endeavors. We developed plans for reconversion, and I sought to explain those plans to workers who were apprehensive about their job security in an economy of peace.

California depends more on Pentagon dollars than any other state. In several speeches there I outlined my plans for reconversion before meetings of workers in defense industries. Their reaction was enthusiastic and encouraging. Meanwhile, the Nixon commercials warned that if workers voted for McGovern, military contracts would be cut back and military bases would be closed down. Many workers did, and after the election many contracts and bases were cut back and closed down. The difference was that under a McGovern administration, there would have been provisions for alternative jobs in peaceful pursuits. The Nixon Administration left displaced workers, with little more than another broken promise.

U.A.W.-I.A.M. Conversion Conference

LOS ANGELES, CALIFORNIA | OCTOBER 16, 1972

There is a concise way to illustrate the choice facing the arms and aerospace workers of California.

Your concern is conversion. And the question is, How do we make a transition from war to peace, without disrupting the lives of workers who depend on defense? How can we put your talents to work not on ways to destroy life abroad, but on programs to lift the quality of life in America?

That is one of the great challenges of our time. It is one that has occupied my attention ever since I entered the United States Senate in 1963. And it is one on which the leadership of the United Auto and Aerospace Workers Union and of the International Association of Machinists have served as a beacon for me and for the country.

The Nixon Administration says it too is concerned about this issue. But consider the priorities set by Mr. Nixon and those around him.

There are 2.7 million people working for the federal government today.

And out of all those people, a grand total of thirteen are working on economic conversion from war to peace.

Mr. Nixon has a White House staff of more than 2,000 people —the largest White House staff in history.

And out of all those people, not a single one is responsible for plans to keep you employed when peace comes.

But if we know what they are not doing, we also have some information on what those Republican politicians think is important.

They hired at least fifty people, at substantial salaries, to sabotage and corrupt our political process. They hired fifty people to conduct some of the shabbiest undercover operations in the history of American politics.

But only thirteen to work on developing peacetime jobs.

According to a report in the *Washington Post* yesterday, there is at least one top aide in the White House, Dwight Chapin, who is responsible for receiving information from that undercover network. The Republican team of saboteurs has a contact who is at Mr. Nixon's elbow every single day—someone who has constant access to the President.

But aerospace workers who are concerned about job security have no contact anywhere in the White House, or even in the Executive Office Building next door.

And I say that is intolerable.

The sad truth is that our government today is so obsessed with political advantage, and so obedient to the privileged few, that it has no time to consider your concerns. And with that kind of administration in power, we will never see the blessings of peace and the security of jobs reunited again.

I propose a different scale of values and a more promising order of business for our country.

I have said in this campaign that my first economic priority is a job for every man and woman who is able to work. On this issue, the choice is clear. For Mr. Nixon's friend, and the chief architect of his economic policy, has declared that full employment in peacetime is a myth.

I have also said in this campaign that while I propose substantial cuts in military spending, I would not eliminate a single job in the arms and aerospace industry until there is another job available to take its place.

That is another issue on which Mr. Nixon and I disagree. For during his term we have seen 1.8 million jobs disappear in defense-related industries—500,000 in aerospace alone. And a big share of those people are still looking for work.

I am fully convinced that both of those commitments—job security in this industry, and a full employment economy—can be met.

For despite all the Republican scare tactics you are seeing in 1972, the truth is that in America today we can find more jobs in peace than in war.

We do not have to send our sons off to fight in order to keep their parents at work. And we do not have to build arms we do not need, in order to have a thriving and prosperous economy for American workers.

Several months ago, I asked a group of distinguished economists to project what would happen if we phased in, over a period of several years, the kind of defense program I have outlined in this campaign. We would adopt a $55 billion military budget by 1975, an amount that is fully adequate to meet our security needs and to fulfill our commitments abroad. And we would apply the savings to domestic needs.

They concluded that by the time the transition was completed, we would have replaced every single job that was lost and added another 1.5 million new jobs besides. They found that just about any other way we spent the savings would produce more jobs than if we left that money in the military budget.

The U.S. Department of Labor has reached a similar conclusion. A recent study by the Bureau of Labor Statistics, "Post-Vietnam Economy, 1975," has affirmed that spending on health, on education, and on other civilian needs will create far more jobs than the same money spent on arms.

What that means in a nutshell is that the father of communism, Karl Marx, was wrong when he said our free economy could not prosper without war.

And it means that the father of Mr. Nixon's latest economic game plan, John Connally, was just as wrong when he said the same thing.

Yet Mr. Nixon's surrogate campaigners are going around the country claiming my program would cost you jobs. They are doing it in speeches, in their television and newspaper propaganda, and in the phony literature that has been circulated in plants here in California.

I do not want to charge that they are lying. Instead, I suspect that they are just too caught up in their own way of thinking.

If this administration had managed to pare $32 billion from the budget over a period of several years, they would probably give most of it away in new tax breaks for big business. And that would certainly produce precious few jobs.

But I would take those funds and invest them immediately in new job-creating enterprises, to deal with the crushing domestic needs that we notice every day of our lives. And for every ten jobs that would be phased out, there would be fifteen new jobs under way.

We would begin that process before the cutbacks occurred.

The first step, in the earliest days of my administration, would be an immediate $10 billion investment in new and rehabilitated housing, transportation, pollution control, and public-service jobs. That would generate about two million new jobs, even before the application of military savings to civilian needs.

As the savings from the arms budget became available, they would be added to the job-creating investment in our own land.

Many of our aerospace workers would be doing precisely the same thing, because much of the arms budget would be preserved. But I also want to use your skills to build natural gas tankers instead of excess destroyers, so we can meet the nation's energy crisis. Instead of working on communications for the Defense Department, you can develop new methods of communication for law enforcement agencies. And there is no reason why the tremendous potential for modern transportation systems is being filled by products made in Germany and Japan instead of in the United States. The facilities and workers of aircraft plants in California can be channeled into developing and building mass-transit systems or modular housing.

With priorities of that kind, I am convinced that we can— and I am determined that we will—build a full employment economy in America, one in which you can count on not only the security of a job, but clean air to breathe, clean water to drink, safe streets to walk on, a decent home you can afford, and dependable transportation to take you back and forth to work.

And let me tell you bluntly what I think of the Republican scaremongers. If anyone comes into your plant and says you will not be able to get and hold a job under these conditions, that person is insulting your intelligence and demeaning your capabilities.

The truth is that your skills and experience would never be

surplus as they are in so many cases now, under an administration that considers the worker expendable. They would instead be held precious, under an administration that would never tolerate the waste of unemployment when there are so many critical jobs to be done.

We need planning and leadership to bridge whatever gap there might be between the old job and the new.

A McGovern administration would insist on reform of pension systems, to provide for early vesting and portability, so you would not lose your retirement rights when you move from one job to another.

And a McGovern administration would insist that if there is any delay between the old job and the new, the country as a whole ought to provide sufficient adjustment benefits to insure against the severe financial hardships that so many aerospace workers are suffering now. The shift to new national priorities is in the national interest, and there is no reason why a small minority—those who have been employed in defense-related industries—must carry the entire cost.

So, again, the issue is sharply drawn between Mr. Nixon and me. As it is in the case of Vietnam, in the case of tax reform, and in so many other issues, it is, as Mr. Nixon has admitted, the "choice of a century."

For you, it is a choice between the constant fear of losing your job, or the security of stable, secure employment.

It is a choice between the frustration of building more overkill, or the satisfaction of work that improves life.

For California, it is a choice between dependence on a rollercoaster military economy, or the prospect of steady growth and prosperity.

And for America, it is a choice between pursuing our worst fears, or realizing our best hopes and our greatest aspirations for a just and decent land.

A Tough, Lean Military

While many veterans disagree with many of its positions on national issues, the Veterans of Foreign Wars nevertheless does represent an important body of opinion in the country, with influence far beyond its own membership rolls. Americans generally are grateful for the sacrifices of those who have gone to battle when the nation called. And despite the growth of cynicism, the great majority of us are still inspired by patriotic themes.

The Nixon campaign appealed to these instincts not by helping those who did fight in Vietnam, but by vilifying those who tried to escape a hated war; not by appealing to true sources of national worth, but by equating patriotism with unquestioning support for bristling piles of weapons. At the VFW convention in Minneapolis, I argued that my defense policies would in the end produce a stronger military, with more certain—and better deserved—public support.

National Convention of Veterans of Foreign Wars

MINNEAPOLIS, MINNESOTA | AUGUST 24, 1972

I come here to present views with which some of you may disagree. But I come as well with a faith that binds us together

—a faith in the free system we all fought to preserve, and in the democracy we would all fight again to defend.

I have come here with a deep concern about the condition of our national security, and about the traditions we want to uphold.

All of us have served in the defense of the United States. I belong, as many of you do, to the age when the Air Force was still in the Army, and the only difference was the amount of the walking.

In our Army not many served because we wanted to spend our lives soldiering. We served because we had a job to do, and we saw that the job we did could make the difference between life and death for our freedom.

Our Army was no band of professional heroes. A few men went over the hill. Others gold-bricked. But in 1944 and 1945 we had another kind of desertion problem. Soldiers were deserting from redeployment depots—the "repple-depples"—to fight with their old units on the front lines.

Our Army left for war amidst the tears of those we left behind. But we knew there would be welcome and honor and a grateful America when we returned. We knew the nation would help us readjust with schooling, with homes, and with jobs. I had a dream of an advanced degree at a great university. But it took the G.I. Bill to make that dream come true.

But things are tragically different today.

In 1970, 65,000 men deserted from the Army. That is enough men to fill about four infantry divisions.

In these last few years, heroin has destroyed far more lives in our Armed Forces than enemy fire. Thousands of Vietnam veterans wander the streets hopelessly addicted to drugs. And a society which had little trouble finding a young man when it wanted to send him off to fight now seems unable to find him when he comes home with poison running through his veins.

An even larger number of young men have returned cursing their entire military experience, and vowing that they will never take up arms again. They have come back not with the satisfaction of a job well done, but with the disillusionment of men who feel their own land has let them down.

And whatever their attitude, they have returned to a society that really does not seem to care.

While we spare no expense on modern gadgets, we somehow cannot find the money to provide veterans' benefits worth more than a fraction of those we received when we came back from World War Two.

Because care and treatment on the battlefield have improved with modern techniques, we find that more of the seriously wounded survive today. But they come back to veterans' hospitals that are understaffed and shamefully neglected. They live out their lives with broken bodies, and with fractured ideals as well.

For all the grand rhetoric we have heard in recent years, joblessness still runs far higher among veterans than among the population as a whole.

I reject the notion that these conditions exist because we have raised a generation of slackers. Our sons are just as good and courageous today as America's sons have ever been.

I think there are other reasons, and I think we delude ourselves if we fail to see them.

One is the longest, most confusing and inconclusive war in our national history.

It is no secret that I have opposed our involvement in Vietnam from the beginning. I have felt that our national interests would be degraded, and our national security would be weakened, by our participation in that war.

We can sense the cost of Vietnam in American blood spilled in a cause we would never win, but could never bring ourselves to leave alone. We can see it in the human wreckage that lies in military hospitals. We may feel it in the long, lonely years of confinement suffered by our prisoners of war—more than eight years, now, for the first American pilot shot down.

But consider, too, the cost to our proud military traditions.

Let me say quite frankly that I think our Armed Forces have

been weakened by the frustration and despair of Indochina. And their morale sinks deeper every month this war goes on in defiance of the will of the American people.

If you doubt that judgment, ask the men who are quitting West Point and the other academies. Ask the enlisted men who are marking time until their tours are up.

We have sent our young men on a mission in which they did not, and could not, believe.

They are told that General Thieu is a friend of the United States. But many of our G.I.'s believe that General Thieu defames almost everything this country stands for.

What kind of a friend would tolerate the rampant graft and corruption and the vicious drug traffic which reaches into the highest levels of Mr. Thieu's government and into the highest command structure of his army? And what friend would tell us, after all the immense sacrifice of this war, that America has not yet done enough on his behalf?

The morale, the pride, the sense of duty and mission which have inspired our Armed Forces—these are precious values. For no matter how impressive our arms, we cannot be militarily strong unless the men and women in our Armed Forces believe in themselves and in their cause.

To retrieve those values we must first place our men, our prisoners, and our hopes for peace ahead of the narrow ambitions of General Thieu. And if Mr. Nixon is going to follow that course anyway, I plead with him to do it now. I plead with him to save the lives and end the confinement for our prisoners by bringing this war to an end now. We should notify General Thieu today that we will no longer underwrite his corrupt regime.

We should stop being controlled by what is best for a dictator in Saigon, and we should stop being controlled by what is asked by dictators in Hanoi. Instead we should start worrying about what is best for America.

Once the war is behind us, we can begin building the kind of hard and tough military force this country needs in a dangerous and troubled world. For the way it is seen by many of its own members is another cause for dissatisfaction and decline in the Armed Forces.

As one who saw the terrible cost of weakness before World War Two, I am deeply committed to a strong military, with all the forces we need to deter nuclear attack and to defend our own society and our vital interests around the world. We must never be so weak as to invite aggression. We must always be strong enough to prevent any threat to our security.

But we must also understand that wasteful spending does not bring real defense. Instead, it only diverts us from the sources of our security—from the modern and effective arms we need, and from the economic and social strength upon which we must draw if we are challenged on the field of battle.

I do not see how it serves our security to have more colonels, Navy captains, generals and admirals now—with two and a half million men under arms—than we had commanding twelve million men at the height of World War Two.

Overall, throughout the Armed Forces, we have one officer or noncommissioned officer to command or supervise every single enlisted man. And in the Army, only one in four men has a job designation with combat skills.

I do not think that is security; I think it is a top-heavy command structure that could easily collapse from the weight of excess brass.

There is an Army vehicle known as "the Goat." It is supposed to cost $5,000 per copy and float. Instead it costs $15,000 per copy and sinks.

Congressman Goldwater recently conducted an investigation of government film-making. He found that the Pentagon has produced and paid for eighteen different films that show you how to brush your teeth.

I do not think that is security; I think it is stupidity—with the taxpayers' dollars.

A few years ago we phased in the M-16 rifle for our combat forces in Vietnam. It kept jamming, and our men found themselves as good as disarmed in the heat of battle. The manufacturer said they were not keeping it clean enough, that it required constant care in the jungle.

Well, I do not think that is security either. And I am sick and tired of our front-line soldiers being used as guinea pigs for weapons that have not been proved.

The Government Accounting Office has recently totaled up more than $35 billion in cost overruns. I think that harms our security, robs the taxpayer, and underwrites sloppy industry management at the same time.

What I have proposed is that we take a hard look at our entire arms establishment from the top to the bottom. I think we will find that there are too many people who are bored in nonproductive jobs. We will find that we have rushed ahead to buy too many weapons that are either unneeded or will not work. And we will find room for savings that will not only allow us to meet some of our accumulated civilian needs, but will help us build a leaner, tougher, and more effective military force as well.

That is the road back to the kind of America we love:

—a land of common purpose, where we can fulfill the promises of freedom;

—a nation whose military power is matched by the power of its ideals;

—a nation where patriotism is not only a recollection of past glories by the old, but the admiration of present works by all of our people of every age;

—and a nation where military service is seen as a high calling, a proud profession, and among the greatest opportunities a free society can offer to its people.

Those are the conditions I want to restore.

So, along with Abraham Lincoln, "Let us strive on . . . to care for him who shall have borne the battle, and for his widow and his orphan—to do all which may achieve and cherish a just and lasting peace among ourselves and with all nations."

The Way to Peace

I remember some resentment against the shorthand term,
"One-issue candidate," which was assigned to me by so
many political writers after I announced my presidential
candidacy in 1971. The one issue was Vietnam. But I did
have a record in other areas, and we had begun the process
of building an unusually comprehensive public platform.

Yet in a very real sense the label was fair. For so many
years I had been heartsick over our involvement in Indochina. For so many years our words and debates and
amendments in the Congress had failed to end this moral
and political outrage. I knew that whoever occupied the
White House could literally end the war, or at least our
involvement, with the stroke of a pen. And that, along with
what this issue said about the nature of the American government, was the greatest single reason for my candidacy.

Television Address

OCTOBER 10, 1972

Tonight, I ask you to think carefully about an issue that has
troubled me more than any other for the last nine years—the
war in Vietnam.

On September 23, 1963, I warned that our deepening involvement in the affairs of the Vietnamese people was "a policy of moral debacle and political defeat."

Under three separate presidents—two of them Democrats and one of them a Republican—I have opposed this war. During these same long years, Mr. Nixon has supported the war. This, I think, is the sharpest and most important difference between Mr. Nixon and me in the 1972 presidential campaign.

Mr. Nixon has described the Vietnam war as our finest hour. I regard it as the saddest chapter in our national history.

Our problem with this terrible war does not stem from the lack of bravery or skill on the part of our fighting men. Indeed, no better American army has ever been sent abroad. Our problem is that we have asked our armed forces to do the impossible—to save a political regime in Saigon that does not even have the respect of its own people. I have been to Vietnam more than once talking to our G.I.'s. They have told me in countless conversations of the frustrating and impossible nature of this assignment.

Before the 1968 election, the Republican candidate, Mr. Nixon, told you that he had a secret plan to end the war. He refused to discuss the details, but he asked your support in the election, and he offered peace in return.

That promise has been broken, and the destruction in Southeast Asia has increased.

The war goes on for our sons who are still ordered into battle. It is true that men have been withdrawn from Vietnam, but half a million American fighting men ranged in the Pacific, Thailand, and Guam are still carrying this war to Vietnam.

Tonight, as I speak to you, some of these men may die. Forty percent of all the Americans lost in Vietnam have died in the last four years—died under the present administration. Since January of 1969, 20,000 young Americans have come home—not in glory, to the cheers of a grateful country, but

My wife inspired a campaign slogan reminiscent of the Roosevelt era: "Put another Eleanor in the White House." While we campaigned together in some cases, as on this whistle-stop railroad tour in the California primary, she had a grueling schedule of her own. Her role as both a campaigner and an adviser went far beyond the traditional practice. She was the first wife of a political candidate to appear on NBC's national interview program Meet the Press, to deal with tough political questions from top professional journalists.

One of the strategy sessions with campaign manager Gary Hart and other members of the staff. Because the days were packed so full, we usually held meetings like this either early in the morning or late at night.

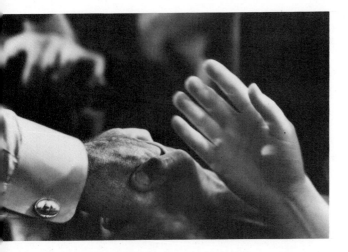

Campaigning.

During the California primary, sizing up the opposition for the fall. President Nixon was reporting on his trip to the Soviet Union, and I was sensing the enormous power of the incumbent to shape news and events in his favor.

The forward cabin of the airplane seemed much more like home than the hotel rooms where we would stop for the night, if only because it remained the same day in and day out. But it was also an office. Around the table from the left are press secretary Dick Dougherty, a senior adviser Fred Dutton, personal aide Jeff Smith, and former Interior Secretary Stewart Udall.

Work on the final draft of my acceptance speech in Miami had to be squeezed in between urgent phone calls and conversations about the selection of a running mate. Our bedroom in the Doral Hotel was the only place with a certain amount of solitude.

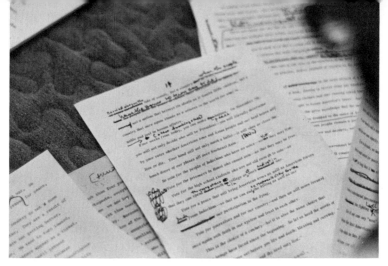

The text of one of the television addresses, about halfway through the writing, rewriting, and editing process.

The campaign was a family affair. Here, between stops, grandson Matthew offers advice on a speech.

A portion of the crowd at a rally in Hartford, Connecticut. Just to my right, in the very front is Lucianne Goldberg, who was exposed in 1973 as one of the agents paid by the Nixon operation to spy on my campaign.

With (seated in front) Jules Witcover of the Los Angeles Times, *now with the Washington* Post, *Walter Mears of the Associated Press; and (back, left to right) James Naughton of the New York* Times, *my executive assistant Gordon Weil, and Peter Lisagor of the Chicago* Daily News. *Beyond their high stature in the press, Witcover, Mears and Naughton became well known for writing irreverent and usually hilarious parodies about the candidate and the campaign.*

Principal collaborators on most of the major speeches were Bob Shrum, John Holum, and Sandy Berger. This was taken about three A.M. in the morning after Election Day, and I had just made some comment about "our words that moved the nation."

in death, to the bitter tears of their families. The secret plan for peace will forever remain a secret to them.

The war goes on also for our prisoners in North Vietnam. Tonight, on the other side of the world, they sit and think of us—of their homes, their families, of children who are growing up without fathers, of a country they may never see again. And in the last four years, 550 more Americans have been taken captive or listed as missing in action, more than 100 of them in the last six months. And if anyone says that the promise to end the war has been kept, let him tell that to the families of the brave men who waste away in the cells of Hanoi. Now, Mr. Nixon says we must bomb and fight to free our prisoners. But just the reverse is true. We must end the bombing and end the fighting, if we are ever to see these prisoners again. Prisoners of war come home when the war ends—not while the war continues.

The war also goes on for the millions of Americans like you who bear its cost. Every single week this war claims $250 million of your taxes. Every week it inflates the cost of everything you buy. Each week it costs $250 million that we need to employ men to rebuild our cities, to fight crime and drugs, to strengthen our schools, and to assist our sick and elderly.

Since he came to the presidency, Mr. Nixon has spent $60 billion of your money on this war—$60 billion of your taxes to kill human beings in Asia instead of protecting and improving human life, in America—$60 billion in the last four years—not for a cause, but for a mistake—not to serve our ideals, but to save the face of our policy-makers.

And the war goes on also for the people of Indochina. Indeed, they are literally being crushed under the weight of the heaviest aerial bombardment the world has ever known. The bombing of Indochina has doubled under the present administration, and while General Thieu is secure in his palace, six million of his fellow Vietnamese are victims—people dead, maimed or driven from their homes. Most of these people are not enemies, but innocents. Our bombs bring them not freedom, but terror. Bombing does not save their land. It destroys it.

The reality of this war is seen in the news photo of the little South Vietnamese girl, Kim, fleeing in terror from her bombed-out school. She has torn off her flaming clothes and she is running naked into the lens of the camera. That picture ought to break the heart of every American. How can we rest with the grim knowledge that the burning napalm that splashed over little Kim and countless thousands of other children was dropped in the name of America?

Now, there are those who say that you will accept this because the toll of suffering now includes more Asians and fewer Americans. But, surely, conscience says to each of us that a wrong war is not made right because the color of the bodies has changed. We are all created in the image of God.

As a bomber pilot in World War Two, like millions of you, I did what had to be done. Our nation took up arms and laid down lives because tyranny threatened all that we held precious. I loved America enough to offer my life in war thirty years ago. And for nine years I have loved this country enough to risk my political life to call us home from a war in Asia that does not serve the interests and the ideals of the American nation.

What, after all, is our purpose in Southeast Asia?

Now, we used to say that we fought in Vietnam to stop Communist China or to stop Communist Russia. But these nations are now quarreling among themselves, and Mr. Nixon's public opinion ratings have gone up after he was wined and dined in the Communist capitals of Peking and Moscow. How can we really argue that it is good to accommodate ourselves to a billion Russian and Chinese Communists—but that we must somehow fight to the bitter end against a tiny band of peasant guerrillas in the jungles of little Vietnam?

Incredible as it seems, when all is said and done, our purpose in Vietnam now comes down to this: Our policy-makers want to save face and they want to save the Saigon regime of General Thieu. Now, that is a fundamental difference between President Nixon and me on the issue in Vietnam. It is a choice, after all, between saving face or saving lives. It is a choice between four more years of war, or four years of peace.

The Nixon position is that the Thieu regime represents self-determination for the people of South Vietnam. Let me tell you what I think his regime represents.

I think our support for General Thieu actually denies the people of South Vietnam the right to choose their own government. The Saigon lawyer, a former president of Rotary International, who had the courage to run against General Thieu four years ago, was sent to jail for five years. Last year, General Thieu issued a decree to force all the other candidates out of the race. This year, he abolished all the local elections, so he could extend his dictatorship to every village in South Vietnam. General Thieu has closed newspapers, simply for printing the truth. He has presided over the execution of 40,000 people without trial on the mere suspicion that they did not support his policies.

The Thieu regime stands for the theft of billions of dollars of our aid, stolen by powerful officials to enrich themselves while their countrymen are in the grip of starvation and disease. And every G.I. who has served in Vietnam knows that is the truth.

Corrupt Vietnamese officials have enriched themselves putting heroin into the veins of a hundred thousand of our G.I.'s. The same poisonous heroin from Southeast Asia is now being shipped into our cities, our suburbs, our streets, and even into the schools of America. And every Vietnam G.I. knows that is true.

This corrupt dictatorship that our precious young men and our tax dollars are supporting cannot be talked clean by official lies. And it cannot be washed clean by American blood. Instead, our own most precious values are corrupted by the very government we fight to defend.

Mr. Nixon would continue the war to preserve General

Thieu's power. On that, he and I disagree. I say: General Thieu is not worth one more American dollar, one more American prisoner, one more drop of American blood.

Mr. Nixon and I also disagree on how to find peace—and this is the second fundamental difference between us.

He has chosen what he calls "decisive military action" to end the fighting. Despite all the highly publicized "secret" meetings with the other side, he has persisted in the belief that we can find peace only in a wider war. But the escalations of 1965 and 1967 were also "decisive military actions" and they did not end the war. They only increased the killing and increased the costs.

Mr. Nixon's invasion of Cambodia, made without the approval of Congress as required by our Constitution—that was a "decisive military action," but it did not end the war. It only brought the war to more people who had been living in peace and it brought Communist rule to two-thirds of that previously neutral country.

The mining of North Vietnamese harbors was a decisive military action, but it did not end the war. The supplies still flow into the South, and our adversary is reported by our own observers to be as strong as ever.

For nearly thirty years, the people of Vietnam have been at war. For nearly thirty years, the Japanese, the French, the Americans have tried "decisive military action" to win a satisfactory peace. And for thirty years, each, in turn, has failed.

Now, the answer to failure is not more of the same. And yet I fear continued war is what the Nixon Administration has in store if they stay in power.

Secretary of Defense Laird recently admitted to a Congressional Committee that the fighting could continue far into the future under present policy.

Four years ago last night, on October 9, 1968, Mr. Nixon, as a candidate for president, said to a crowd in California—and I quote: "Those who have had a chance for four years and could not produce peace should not be given another chance."

Now, Mr. Nixon has had his chance. He could not produce peace in four years. And we have every indication that he cannot produce peace in eight years.

So, I ask the American people: Shall we break free at last from General Thieu? Shall we forget about saving face and begin saving the soul of our nation? Shall we demonstrate that we are determined to stop the killing and to stand for peace? My answer is: Yes.

Let me now set forth the specific steps that I would take as president to carry out that determination.

Immediately after taking my oath as president, if the war has not ended by then, I would issue a national security directive to the secretary of defense, to the joint chiefs of staff, and to our commands in the field, with the following orders:

—Immediately stop all bombing and acts of force in all parts of Indochina;

—Immediately terminate any shipments of military supplies that continue the war;

—Immediately begin the orderly withdrawal of all American forces from Vietnam, from Laos and Cambodia, along with all salvageable American military equipment. And we will assign whatever transportation is required to complete that process and to complete it within ninety days—a time period that I have been told by competent military authority is well within our capability.

Second, I would issue the following instructions to our negotiators in Paris:

—Notify the representatives of the other side that we have taken these steps to end the hostilities, and that we now expect that they will accept their obligation under their own Seven Point Proposal of 1971—to return all prisoners of war and to account for all missing in action. We will expect that process to be completed within ninety days to coincide with our complete withdrawal from the war.

—We would further notify all parties that the United States will no longer interfere in the internal politics of Vietnam, and that we will allow the Vietnamese people to work out their own settlement. The United States is prepared to cooperate to see that any settlement, including a coalition government, gains international recognition.

Third, I would send the vice-president to Hanoi to speed the arrangements for the return of our prisoners and an accounting of the missing. I would also instruct our diplomats to contact the opposing parties in Laos and Cambodia in order to secure release of prisoners held in those countries, and an accounting of missing in action, including American civilian newsmen now missing in Cambodia. There are six known prisoners in Laos, and nearly three hundred missing. No effort has been made to secure their release.

Fourth, after all of our prisoners have been returned, and we have received a satisfactory accounting for any missing men, I would order the secretary of defense and the joint chiefs to close our bases in Thailand, to bring home any troops and equipment still there, and to reassign elsewhere any ships still stationed in the waters adjoining Indochina.

Fifth, as the political solution in Vietnam is worked out by the Vietnamese themselves, we should join with other countries in repairing the wreckage left by this war.

Sixth, I would ask the Congress to take immediate action on an expanded program for our veterans. I think it is simply a disgrace that our government is able to find these young men to send off to war, but somehow we look the other way when they come back in need of an education or decent medical treatment or a decent job.

Now, like many other veterans of World War Two, I received a four-year education under a generous G.I. Bill of Rights. I think Vietnam veterans need that help more than those of us who fought a generation ago because we came back with the welcome of a nation that knew we had fought and won a necessary war. The Vietnam veterans come back to a country that largely believes this war was a mistake. So, we ought to literally put the arms of this nation around these young men and guarantee them either a good job or a fully funded higher education. Months ago, I sponsored in the Senate a Vietnam Veterans Bill of Rights that would do precisely that.

Finally, when the war has ended, when our troops and prisoners are home, and when we have provided for the veterans of Vietnam, we must then consider the young men who chose jail or exile because they could not in conscience fight in this war. So, following the example of earlier presidents, I would give these young men the opportunity to come home. Personally, if I were in their position, I would volunteer for two years of public service on subsistence pay simply to demonstrate that my objection was not to serving the nation, but to participating in a war I thought was morally wrong.

We are not a vindictive or mean-spirited people. And we must act as Lincoln told us—"with malice toward none and charity for all." We must bind up the wounds of this nation, and we must bring all of our sons back. In that same spirit, we must oppose any so-called war-crimes trials to fix the blame for the past on any citizen or any group of citizens. Vietnam has been a terrible experience for all of us, on every side of this issue. And this is not the time for recrimination. It is the time for reconciliation.

So, this is what I would do to bring America home from a hated war. And it is a program that will work. The people of France were once trapped in Vietnam, even as we are. But in 1954 they chose a new president, Pierre Mendès-France, whose highest commitment was to achieve peace in Indochina. His program was very similar to mine. And within just five weeks, the war was over. Within three months, every last French prisoner had been returned.

Now, I ask you to remember that I speak to you as one who has publicly opposed this war for nine years. I ask you to remember that my opponent has supported American military intervention in Vietnam ever since 1954. I ask you to recognize that every detail of my position is fully out in the open. It is a public plan—not a secret plan.

Often during this last tortured decade, I have reflected on a question from the Scriptures: "Which of us, if his son asked him for bread, would give him a stone?" Our sons have asked for jobs—and we have sent them to an Asian jungle. Our sons have asked for an education—and we have taught them how to kill. Our sons have asked for a full measure of time—and 50,000 of them have been lost before their time.

So, let us seize the chance to lift from our sons and ourselves the terror of this war, and bestow the blessings of peace. And then we can restore our sense of purpose and our character as a great nation.

This is not just a question of material wealth—although the billions which would otherwise be lost in Southeast Asia could then be used to secure a better life for our own people. But more important for America, there will be a special healing in the wings of peace. It will be a healing of our doubts and a rekindling of our faith in this great and good land, and in our own capacity to make it so.

On the night when the last American soldier from Vietnam has landed in San Francisco, there will be a new birth of confidence and hope for all of us. On that night, we will know that, once free of the waste of this war, we can begin the rebuilding of our own land—a task that can provide a fulfilling job for every man and woman in America who is able to work. On that night, America can begin to be America again. It can be the America that we learned to love in the days of our youth—a country that once again stands as a witness to the world for what is noble and just in human affairs.

This is the choice of a century. But it is also the same choice that human beings have faced from the very beginning. So, let us heed the ancient words: "I have set before you life and death, blessing and cursing. Therefore, choose life, that thou and thy seed may live."

Thank you. God bless you.

They, Too, Are Created
in the Image of God

The impression was widespread among political experts that opposition to the war would recede as American casualties were reduced. Subsequent events, particularly the congressional prohibition of bombing in Cambodia, have proved that we are a more decent nation than the skeptics claimed. I spoke of that decency many times in the campaign, and of the immorality of substituting our bombs for the bodies of our sons. My message was simple and deeply felt—it was as wrong to kill others in an unjust cause as it was to sacrifice American soldiers.

LOS ANGELES, CALIFORNIA | SEPTEMBER 26, 1972

Over the last twenty months, I have been campaigning for the presidency in one of the longest formally announced campaigns in the history of this country. During all that time, I have given attention to the whole range of domestic problems that face our country—the problems of unemployment, problems of inflation and mismanagement of the economy, the misdirection of the priorities of the nation, the loss of confidence and credibility in our government, and the erosion of our constitutional safeguards.

In all of these areas I have offered alternatives to the American people. I have offered something else besides the sterile Republican rallying cry—"four more years."

But there is one concern that surpasses all the others. And that matter has weighed on my conscience for almost nine years, and for all that time it has literally been an obsession with me. And now that issue forces us to ask more directly and more insistently than any other, these questions: What kind of country is it we intend to be? What is it we want to stand for in the world? And how would we like to be remembered when the history of our time is written?

During the hour we meet here tonight, one hundred thousand pounds of deadly bombs will fall on the people of Southeast Asia.

As I speak to you tonight, hundreds of American pilots and airmen are confined to prison cells in Hanoi. Some of them have been in those cells for more than eight years—for longer than it took for America to win her independence.

Nearly 150,000 Americans are still mired down in this war. The President talks about winding it down. He has withdrawn forces from Vietnam. But those 150,000, in Vietnam and offshore and in Thailand and in Guam, have a direct assignment to continue the combat in Indochina. They are still ground down in that bitter struggle.

And as I speak, thousands of Asians are burning, bleeding, and dying under the bombs that fall from American planes. They suffer in a struggle most of them will never understand. Many of them are innocent children, many are the old—but none of them have direct responsibility for the conflict that takes their lives.

I want you to know tonight that every fiber of my being, every ounce of moral sense that I possess, is determined to do whatever we have to do in 1972 to see that we do not have four more years of this barbarism.

Now, in the presidential campaign of 1968, the Republican presidential candidate said, in his most serious tones, that he had a plan for peace. He said that once the campaign was over his plan would be unveiled. And then he added, on October 9, 1968—almost four years ago: "Those who have had the chance for four years and could not produce peace should not be given another chance."

Today that candidate is president of the United States. And his four years are up.

But his secret plan will remain forever a secret in the hearts of 20,000 Americans who were alive at the time that plan was announced and who are no longer with us. It remains a secret to countless thousands of human beings in these little countries in Southeast Asia who have remained under aerial and artillery bombardment since January of 1969.

What is it that keeps a great and decent country like the United States involved in this cruel killing and destruction? Why is it that we cannot find the wit and the will to escape from this dreadful conflict that has tied us down for so long?

We are told first of all that the bombing continues and our military presence continues in order to rescue the prisoners of war. But what a transparent fraud that is.

Just a few days ago, the one hundredth American in the last five months was blasted out of the sky over North Vietnam. In fact, more than five hundred airmen have become prisoners or missing in action since Mr. Nixon set out on this course to free the prisoners of war.

Surely, we can all see that bombing does not release prisoners, but only makes more prisoners with each passing day. It will make new prisoners of men who at this very moment are now free—men who have not yet been sent out on the mission that will take their liberty away.

Last Christmas, the wife of a missing American pilot, Major William Mullens, wrote about her fifth bleak Christmas alone. Listen to her words:

"Christmas is pain and lonely and tears; and he'll be away for many more years . . .

"Don't think about Asians, or question why; prisoners alone and forgotten should die . . .

"Talk of brotherhood and kindness and cheer; tell all your friends it's been a good year . . .

"Peace on earth is a lie, and death is sadness; they'll never be back, for mankind is madness."

Only one thing will bring these prisoners of war back, and that is to end this murderous war in Southeast Asia.

Last week, I had a brief argument with a young man at a Western Electric plant in Columbus, Ohio. He was one of many Americans who have been told, and I suspect he sincerely believes, that we are staying in Vietnam, and that the bombers go out day after day, on behalf of self-determination and freedom for the people of Vietnam. But what a tragic deception that is.

General Thieu's brand of freedom means jail for anyone who has the audacity to tell the truth about what is going on in South Vietnam.

It means if you have the courage to run against him for the presidency, as a lawyer named Dzu did four years ago, you go to the penitentiary after the election. It means forcing a law through his puppet assembly to disqualify all the other candidates in the most recent campaign.

His brand of democracy recently has meant suspending the electoral process and local control in ten thousand villages across the face of South Vietnam. And anyone who is even vaguely aware of the importance of village life to the people of that part of the world knows what a cruel and terrible blow this is to the whole political and social structure of South Vietnam.

Mr. Thieu's brand of democracy means closing down the newspapers anytime an editor has the courage to suggest that there might be something wrong in the administration of Saigon.

General Thieu's brand of self-determination means executing more than 38,000 of his fellow countrymen without a trial, on suspicion that they do not support the government.

It means a government that literally seethes with corruption

—with officials who steal our aid and who are deeply involved in the hard-drug traffic that has sent poisonous, killing heroin into the veins of a hundred thousand American G.I.'s. And those same Southeast Asian drugs are now flowing into this country, not only killing our people or destroying their lives, but causing at least 50 percent of the crime that makes it unsafe to be on the streets at night.

Mr. Nixon told us last week about his plan to cut off military and economic aid to any government that traffics in hard drugs. I would suggest that the place to begin is with his friend, General Thieu, in Saigon.

Then we are told there is a third reason why we are in Vietnam. We are told that the bombs fall so that America's honor will be preserved.

But how many of us know what is really happening to the honor of America in Southeast Asia? How many of us know how our moral posture in the world has suffered because of the terrible death and killing that goes on in the name of America?

It is a fact that American casualties are down and the economic costs have been somewhat reduced. But another kind of cost has escalated.

The war now, more than at any stage since we have been in Southeast Asia, has become an assault on the decency and self-respect of the people of this great country.

For what we now present to the world is the spectacle of a rich and powerful nation standing off at a safe distance and raining down a terrible technology of death on helpless people below—the most incredible and murderous bombardment in all the history of mankind.

Almost four million tons of bombs have been dropped since 1969—more than all the bombs unleashed in all theaters in World War Two and Korea combined.

All of that has been done in the name of saving South Vietnam. Yet the tragic irony is that most of the victims are those same South Vietnamese people we say we are there to defend.

Enemy soldiers know how to avoid the bombs. They move at night and hide by day. They stay out in the jungles where even the smart bombs cannot find them.

But there are 20 million bomb craters scarring the face of South Vietnam.

There are 400,000 innocent civilians dead—old men, women, and children. And all of them are South Vietnamese.

There are 900,000 civilians wounded—all South Vietnamese.

There are 6.3 million refugees living in hovels and dying from hunger and disease. They are all South Vietnamese, and they represent about a third of the population of that land.

We seem to be saying that one man killed is murder, but thousands killed is only a statistic.

We have counted bodies so long that somehow they just don't seem to count any more at all.

Perhaps we need to hear how this war seems to the people who are on the receiving end. Listen to this young father in Laos:

"My son is six years old. We are from Ban Qui. In July 1969 we were all sitting in our little shelter out in the forest when the planes came. Two people with us—a man aged sixty and a little girl aged seven—were killed lying in their beds. My little son's hand was hit, and his fingers flew up, imbedding themselves in the roof of our shelter."

The air strikes come with new weapons and new techniques, and these weapons have a very special purpose. They cannot blow up a bridge. They cannot destroy a structure. They do not stop a truck or even penetrate a rubber tire. Many of them have only one purpose, and that is to kill and maim human beings.

We have the innocuous sounding "pineapple" with 250 steel pellets in the casing of each one. A single aircraft carries 1,000 of these "pineapples," or 250,000 pellets, and it can saturate an area the size of four football fields. And it just hits people.

We have developed a way to explode those weapons above the ground, so they can even reach people who hide in ditches or holes.

We have steel fleshettes that penetrate the skin and cannot be removed. We have napalm—jellied gasoline that sticks to the skin as it burns. We have white phosphorus that cannot be extinguished until it burns itself out.

Now, these are some of the weapons that produced that picture we saw in the press not too long ago of the little girl, Kim, running away from a school that had been hit by American napalm. She was naked, her clothing had been inflamed, her flesh was burned, and she was running directly into the lens of a cameraman nearby.

And I want to say to my fellow Americans that that picture ought to break the heart of the people of America.

Can we ever comprehend the horror? Can we ever understand the anguish of a mother who watches her child torn apart before her eyes, of a father whose family disappears forever beneath tons of earth?

I do not charge that we are deliberately pounding innocent civilians in Indochina. That is not my claim.

But what I ask is this: Does it make any difference whether it is deliberate or not? On the ground, the suffering is no less if it is inflicted by accident instead of design. And our most sincere apology will not resurrect the dead.

I was a bomber pilot in World War Two. We fought then, and many died, to defeat a vicious tyranny that threatened the world. If need be, we would do it again.

But how can we tolerate today's awful destruction, when we know its only purpose is to preserve one kind of tyranny against another?

How can we tolerate it, when we know that where we once destroyed a village in order to save it, we will soon complete the destruction of an entire land?

So I ask here tonight how our honor is saved by fewer American deaths, and more Asian. I ask if we are more honorable because the color of the corpses has changed from white to yellow.

I think not, for the blood is still red.

I think not, because when we think of the people of Indo-china we must know that they, too, are created in the image of God. . . .

Our children look to us for moral guidance—for America's true ideals. But we protect the prestige of warmakers. And we pay with the soul of our nation.

The war does not represent the honor of America, and it does not represent the American people.

I have traveled this land for twenty months, in a quest for the presidency and in a search for peace.

I have looked into the eyes of people all across America. I have listened to what they had to say, and I have tried to sense what was in their hearts.

What I have found is that the American people remain a powerful moral force—a force for compassion and love and human decency, not only in our own land, but throughout the world.

And I have found that the American people have a common hunger to love their country, to take pride in what it does, and to honor what it represents. They want to stand up once again for the ideals which gave America birth two hundred years ago.

That is a goal I share.

That is the reason for my firm pledge that the bombs will stop falling on Indochina—and we will begin the withdrawal of all our remaining forces—on the very day of my inauguration.

On that same day, we will work to arrange the release of our prisoners of war, so they can all be returned along with our forces within ninety days.

We will end our military support of the corrupt regime in Saigon, so the people of Vietnam will be able at last to choose their own future.

And then we will resolve that never again will we commit the young blood of America to bail out a corrupt dictatorship half a world away.

So I ask you to come with me, and we will restore peace.

Come with me, and we will find again the true patriotism that has nourished our freedom for two centuries.

Come with me, and we will bring America home to the great and good and decent land our people want it to be.

Peace: Not at Hand

On October 26 Henry Kissinger announced, not peace, but peace "at hand." After ten years of opposition to the war, years of false promises and betrayed hopes, I was skeptical of this election eve "progress report." We convened in Grand Rapids for several hours of discussion and a night of writing, and the next day I expressed my reaction to the Kissinger briefing in another nationwide television speech. It reflects my resolution that, even if we were fated to lose the election, we would so conduct ourselves in the closing hours of the campaign that the Administration would then and later feel the utmost pressure to redeem the promise of peace.

Radio and Television Address

NOVEMBER 3, 1972

I want to talk with you tonight about two events that occurred last night. The first was President Nixon's paid political broadcast, in which he discussed the Vietnam negotiations. He admitted that he has rejected the settlement his own negotiator accepted nearly a month ago. He did not say when there would be an agreement. And he withdrew the latest promise of peace.

So this past week has become another week when the war was not ended. We were told that peace was at hand. But then the hand that could have signed that peace pushed it aside.

The second event last night occurred in Michigan. I was on television answering questions from people who called on the phone. After the program, we received a call from Mr. Charles Stewart of Gladstone, Michigan.

His son, an Army enlisted man, was killed in Vietnam two days ago. He died on the day the peace was supposed to be signed. He was nineteen. He died on the day Mr. Nixon decided to continue fighting the war, while fighting over what he calls the "details" of peace.

Charles Stewart, Jr., died for those "details." And he was not alone. This week twenty-two other Americans died for the same "details."

For the sake of those "details," the bombs still fall, the guns still fire, and the terrible pain goes on.

Even as I speak to you, human lives are being lost in a war that is wrong. More parents learn each week the terrible sorrow of burying their own sons.

But now we have learned something else.

Charles Stewart, Jr., and all the others are not really dying for details, but for a deception.

The President may say peace, peace—but there is no peace, and there never was.

For it is not the details, but the central issues that are still in dispute.

I know that many Americans were struck by the coincidence that after four years of fighting and dying, the Administration announced just twelve days before the election that peace was in reach. We wondered why a settlement that was unsatisfactory until now was embraced at the end of this campaign.

But, like you, I wanted deeply to believe what we were told. If you know my record of opposition to this war for more than nine years, through both Democratic and Republican administrations, then you also know that I would rather have peace than a campaign issue.

So I welcomed Dr. Kissinger's announcement last Thursday. I welcomed the news that an agreement was just a few minor matters away.

But now this hope is betrayed. We see now that when the President's most important adviser announced that peace had come, it was actually a deception designed to raise our hopes before we went to vote on Tuesday.

This is blunt language and a strong accusation. I am sorry to say it, but I believe it to be true.

I ask you to judge for yourselves. I ask you to hear Mr. Nixon's own words, to heed his record, and then to decide if he has been fair and open with the people.

In 1968, the American people voted to end the war. Mr. Nixon was elected on a promise of peace. And since then, every measure of public opinion has carried a rising cry for peace.

In 1969, the central issue was whether to seek a military victory for General Thieu or peace for the American people.

The basis for successful negotiations was already there.

The other side wanted elections, conducted not by General Thieu but by an independent coalition group.

General Thieu wanted continued war, to preserve his power unchallenged. He said he would never accept a deadline, that he would never allow a coalition, and that he would never permit peace until he had won.

Mr. Nixon chose General Thieu. And he began his term with the same discredited policy that had failed before—that had failed for the French and failed for us. He thought peace could be won through more war, through invasions and incursions, through bombs and bullets and blood.

With Senator Hatfield and other members of the Congress, Republicans and Democrats alike, I sponsored legislation to bring the peace that was promised. We proposed a deadline to end the bombing and to bring our troops and prisoners home, to leave Vietnam, and to leave it to the Vietnamese to work out their own peace.

This proposal had the support of three-quarters of the American people. But when it appeared that it might pass, Mr. Nixon disclosed that he was engaged in secret discussions with the North Vietnamese. He told us he was searching for peace in the conference room, and that the Congress should not interfere.

That disclosure did not hasten an agreement in Paris. All it did was to stifle the demand for peace at home. And that is why it was made.

Mr. Nixon's policy did not change. He involved Cambodia to capture a central Vietcong command center that did not exist. He sent armies into Laos that were hurled back in defeat and despair. He bombed more relentlessly than ever. He mined North Vietnamese harbors, seeking an impossible victory through reckless acts of war.

But to placate the American people, he pretended he was making peace. As the bombs kept falling, Dr. Kissinger kept traveling. The secret meetings suddenly became highly publicized meetings, to make sure you knew they were taking place as the election approached.

We have challenged that charade in this campaign. We have reminded candidate Nixon of his own words in 1968—that "those who have had a chance for four years, and could not produce peace, should not be given another chance." And I have set before the American people, not a secret plan, but an open plan to end the war.

Mr. Nixon apparently feared that challenge. So on October 8, Dr. Kissinger agreed in a closed meeting to accept the settlement the other side wanted—on almost the same terms they offered four years ago.

North Vietnamese forces would stay in the South.

Elections would be arranged by a coalition—by Communists, by neutralists, and by representatives of the Saigon regime—to assure that General Thieu could not dictate the results.

American bombing would stop, American forces would

leave, and American prisoners would be freed—all within a period of sixty days.

Mr. Nixon's representative agreed to all of this on October 8. And he agreed, too, on when the settlement would be signed —October 31, one week before the election.

That was no arbitrary deadline, as Mr. Nixon pretended last night.

It was an agreed-upon deadline, set by both sides together. Now it had passed.

And there was no "major breakthrough" for peace, as Mr. Nixon also pretended last night.

Instead, there has been a fatal breakdown on the central issues. Now this chance for an agreement is gone.

Dr. Kissinger took the agreement to General Thieu. And General Thieu said no.

Dr. Kissinger took the agreement to President Nixon. And President Nixon said no.

What Dr. Kissinger accepted and what Mr. Nixon and General Thieu rejected was a coalition to set up the elections, and American withdrawals without a mutual withdrawal by North Vietnam.

Those are the conditions General Thieu has always rejected. And because they are not resolved, as Mr. Nixon admits, we have changed nothing in the last four years.

Now someone must answer for 20,000 more American dead, for 110,000 more wounded, for 550 more captured or missing, for $60 billion more wasted in the last four years.

And now someone must answer for the cruel political deception of these past several weeks.

On October 11, when the agreement was still secret, I addressed the nation on Vietnam.

I spelled out what I saw as the greatest single roadblock to peace—Mr. Nixon's unfailing acceptance of General Thieu's orders; his willingness to place the power of this corrupt dictator ahead of freedom for our prisoners, life for our soldiers, and an end to the war.

I also outlined my program for peace. It called for an end to the bombing, an end to the shelling, and withdrawal in ninety days' time. It accepted the North Vietnamese offer to free our prisoners as we withdraw.

Republican politicians ridiculed that proposal. They said it was "unrealistic," and they called it "surrender."

But that was not true, and they knew it.

Three days before I spoke, Dr. Kissinger had already embraced the same principles in private, in discussion with North Vietnam. But they called that "peace with honor"—the same results they called "surrender," just a few days before.

So what can we conclude today?

After four years of war, Mr. Nixon has closed the door to peace once again. If he escapes his responsibility now, do you think he will end the war after the election, once he is free from the will of the American people?

We know, too, that the war can be ended in a matter of hours, on the terms I have already proposed. If General Thieu says we cannot dictate peace to him, we need a president who will reply: "General Thieu, you are not going to dictate any more war for us."

Mr. Nixon will never say that. I will.

Mr. Nixon will never sign the agreement. I will.

Mr. Nixon will not end the war. It will be my very first act.

Now we must draw the painful conclusion that the events of recent weeks were not a path to peace, but a detour around Election Day. The officials who are sworn to serve you instead have sought to mislead you for their own political gain. Their strategy was designed to create the illusion of peace from Thursday, October 26—when Dr. Kissinger made his announcement —until Tuesday, November 7—when you will make your decision about the next president of the United States.

In a campaign marked by falsehood, sabotage, secret funds, special-interest deals, and criminal activity, this is the worst deceit of all. They have played politics with the Justice Department, the FBI, the Supreme Court, and even the Constitution.

Now they play politics with our prisoners and our soldiers and life itself. It is they who treat our men like toy soldiers, to be knocked over by the hand that should protect them.

What we are seeing in this campaign is the manipulation of our hopes by men who know how to get power and want to keep it, but do not know what it is for. In politics, there are some things more precious than victory. One of them is truth.

But these men will say anything to win.

They will say that there is peace even in the midst of war. They will say that inflation is cut in half when in fact it is as high as it was before. They will say that the tide has been turned against crime when crime is at the highest tide in history.

But the truth is all around us. Ask the families of our prisoners if the fighting has ended. Ask a housewife if the cost of living is under control. Ask yourselves if you feel safe on a city street at night.

And ask yourselves if you really believe the incredible attacks on the Democratic Party in 1972. They are part of the same technique of fear and innuendo Mr. Nixon has used so often before—against Harry Truman, Congressman Voorhees, Helen Gahagan Douglas, and Adlai Stevenson, against Lyndon Johnson and Hubert Humphrey, and John and Robert Kennedy. This year, for example, Mr. Nixon tells you that the programs I have proposed would mean a 50 percent increase in federal taxes. That is a lie—and the President knows it.

He made the same charge at the Republican Convention— and when the press asked Administration officials to prove it, they could not even explain it.

I am tired of answering the same old lies.

I am tired of the lie that my economic proposals will put half the country on welfare. The truth is that they will reduce welfare by 30 percent and put the nation back to work.

I am tired of answering the lie that my tax reform will increase the taxes of working people and ordinary citizens, when the truth is that it will not take a single penny more from Ameri-

cans who live on wages or salaries. Indeed, it will cut your property taxes at least by a third.

Mr. Nixon knows what my positions really are. But he does
not want you to know. Why do you think he is so afraid to
come out of the White House and meet me like a man, in face-
to-face debate? Why is he so anxious to falsify my views? Why
is he so unwilling to make his charges in front of me, where no
distortion will go unchallenged?

The answer is clear. Mr. Nixon and his campaigners are trying to trick you into voting against yourself. They understand
how you will vote when you learn what I want to do, and what
they have done.

And what they have done with the war in Vietnam is the
worst of their deeds.

That is why peace remains the overriding issue. For without
peace, there will be no reduction in the cost of living. There will
be no full employment. There will be no renewal of our purpose
as a nation. And there will be no life at all for so many
among us.

If Mr. Nixon disagrees with the main thrust of my remarks
here this evening, I urge that we go together before the American people and clarify our differences on the issues tomorrow
or Sunday, or even Monday, evening.

At this late stage of the campaign, it is past time he quit
hiding behind his so-called surrogates or aides like Mr. Kissinger.
Mr. Nixon is responsible for his own policies. He is the one who
should reply on these crucial issues—not Mr. Kissinger. He is
the one who should defend and clarify the issues in public
debate with me—not Mr. Kissinger or some other aide.

I do not honestly know whether the war weighs as deeply on
the minds of the American people as it does on mine. I do not
honestly know whether the blunt words I have said tonight will
help me or hurt me in this election. I do not really care.

For almost a decade, my heart has ached over the fighting
and the dying in Vietnam. I cannot remember a day when I did

not think of this tragedy. I can remember every picture of a bombed-out school or a napalmed child, and every letter from a family in South Dakota who lost their son. I remember the campaign of 1968, when we heard of a promise of peace. And I worry that unless this country votes for peace now, in the next campaign, in 1976, we will still be working out the "details" of a war that has gone on four more years.

I think of the words of Valerie Kuschner, whose husband has been a prisoner since 1967. "My husband," she said, "has already had his four more years."

Yet many of you wonder whether there really is another choice. Millions are confused and doubtful and suspicious of any candidate who pledges peace.

What can I tell you?

I can only say that there is no way I could continue a war I have hated from the beginning.

And this is the sharpest difference between Mr. Nixon and me. He has always supported that war. I have opposed it.

He has called Vietnam our finest hour. I have called it the saddest chapter in our national history.

He will not set a date for peace. As president, I will bring all of our troops and all of our prisoners home within ninety days of my inauguration.

This Tuesday will be a day of reckoning for America.

It will be the day when we decide between war and peace.

The Scripture says: "I have set before you life and death, blessing and cursing; now choose life so that thou and thy seed may live."

Thank you and God bless you.

A Balanced Economy

A number of my supporters tell me in retrospect that I never should have changed the "$1,000 Plan." They have a point. The plan was a complicated but basically sound idea. Yet it was also politically disastrous and maddeningly difficult to explain in the midst of a campaign. The misperceptions and misconceptions of it simply could not be laid to rest, no matter how hard we tried.

In the end, I offered a different plan to accomplish the same objectives—taking people out of poverty and taking the nation out of the welfare mess. More significantly, I outlined the most comprehensive tax reforms ever proposed in a presidential campaign.

My views on both tax reform and welfare reform were presented in a speech to the Security Analysts Society on Wall Street. Probably no speech of the entire campaign was so carefully researched, written, and revised.

New York Society of Security Analysts

NEW YORK CITY | AUGUST 29, 1972

I am grateful for this opportunity to share my views with you. Your profession as security analysts requires that you look beyond lables and first impressions to find the facts. Today I ask that you extend your expertise from portfolios to politics.

In 1932, an incumbent Republican president said that "the only possibility of winning the election is . . . exciting a fear of what Roosevelt would do."

In 1972, Richard Nixon has adopted a similar strategy. His acceptance speech offered no accounting of his stewardship; it summoned no vision for the future. Instead, the President of the United States sounded a call to fear.

Last week, he tried to make the American people afraid that a Democratic administration would abandon our prisoners of war. But it is in fact his policy of endless bombing which abandons so many of our sons to endless bondage.

Last week, he tried to make the American people afraid that a Democratic president would undermine national security. But my alternative defense budget would eliminate the fat—not the muscle—and leave us with a military system capable of destroying any adversary twenty times over.

Last week, he tried to make the American people afraid that Democrats do not respect law and order. But it is in fact Richard Nixon who has demeaned our highest court of law with shoddy nominations, two of which were rejected by the United States Senate. And agents of his "law and order" campaign have been arrested with their wiretap equipment, invading the Democratic National Committee in the dark of night. According to findings of the U.S. General Accounting Office, other Nixon agents seem to be presiding over questionable and unreported political slush funds many times the size of the $18,000 fund that nearly removed Mr. Nixon from his place on the national ticket in 1952.

In our political system, there are things more precious than partisan victory. One of them is the truth.

And nowhere was truth more the victim of partisanship— nowhere did the President speak last week with less regard for the facts—than in his distorted indictment of Democratic economic policy. He concluded a long list of fantastic and groundless charges by shouting: "We cannot and will not let them do this to America."

But what have the Nixon-Agnew Republicans done to America in the past four years?

They say they stand for full employment—but they have added two million workers to the unemployment rolls.

They say they stand for a balanced budget—but their deficits have already exceeded the combined deficits of President Eisenhower, President Kennedy, and President Johnson. Indeed, the cumulative four-year Nixon deficit of $80 billion represents a fifth of the entire national debt accumulated since the age of George Washington.

They say they stand for stable prices—but consumer prices have risen eighteen points while they have been in power.

They say they stand for free enterprise—but in just three and a half years we have lurched from an invitation to business and labor to ignore wage and price guidelines, to an abrupt wage-price freeze, and then to wage and price controls.

And they say they stand for American success in the field of foreign trade—but in 1971 we experienced the first trade deficit in this century, and it will be even larger this year.

I can understand why the Republicans would prefer to forget their own economic record.

Their attempt to cover up their failures with a call to fear the Democrats serves narrow political purposes. But it is no service to America.

This year, such scarce tactics are doubly dangerous. Not only do they obscure the judgments we must make about the past; they also divert us from the difficult choices ahead.

Because the tax cuts of 1969 and 1971 combined with unemployment have drained federal revenue, because automatic increases in government programs will diminish federal resources still further, and because we have been saddled with crushing military expenditures, there is simply no money for new federal initiatives unless we set new federal priorities. President Nixon deals with this harsh fact by ignoring it. In his acceptance speech, he talked about higher retirement benefits—but he did not tell us how he would pay the bill. He talked about reducing property taxes—but he did not tell us how he would replace the revenue. In this election year, he promises aid to parochial schools, but we have seen neither his plan nor its financing. He hails an arms reduction agreement with Russia but then asks the Congress to increase military spending by $4 billion. For four years he has talked about revenue sharing with cities and states, but he has not provided the revenue to share. For four years, he has talked of Family Assistance, but he has shown more vigor in vetoing child-development and education bills than in pressing for Family Assistance. And if we do the things he suggests without sounding financing, we will strengthen the already harsh grip of inflation on the families of America.

We cannot do what we want to do unless we do what we have to do. We must raise additional funds in a fair and equitable way—and we must cut the waste from the federal budget in a prudent and efficient way. We must exercise the fiscal responsibility of explaining how we will finance every single program we propose.

So what I offer is a balanced full-employment economy—where we can provide enough both to protect our interest abroad and to bring progress at home. What I offer is not simply a set of promises, but a specific plan to pay for those promises.

First, I would reduce by approximately $10 billion in each of the next three years the rapidly escalating, lavish Nixon military budget.

This reduction is safe and sensible. Current military spending wastes billions of dollars on planes that do not fly, missiles that will not work, and more top brass to command two and a half million men today than we had to command twelve million men at the end of World War Two. It includes money for arms we do not need and a capacity to fight guerrilla conflicts that are none of our business. It includes 500,000 American troops and dependents in Europe—a number more than double the level President Eisenhower thought adequate.

I will never permit America to become a second-rate power in the world. Neither can we permit America to become a second-rate society. And if we choose a reasonable military budget, we will not have to choose between the decline of our security and the deterioration of our standard of life. A nation does not live by weapons alone—and the waste of scarce wealth on excess firepower will finally make us, not a stronger nation, but a beleaguered fortress groaning under the dead weight of excessive arms and a demoralized military bureaucracy.

America's security includes not only the power of our weapons, but the prosperity of our economy, the progress of our society, and the credibility of our government. Does anyone doubt that all of these have been weakened in recent years? Do we remember General Eisenhower's warning in 1961 that if the military takes too much, it weakens the nation by undermining other areas of national strength?

So let us compare fact with fear and the Nixon military budget with the McGovern budget.

Both provide overwhelming power to defend the United States, our vital allies, and our vital interests. The McGovern budget would accomplish that for considerably less than the Nixon budget. Instead of the projected escalation in the Nixon budget, I propose carefully justified reductions based on a more critical look at our real defense needs.

The Nixon budget spends money to prepare for more Vietnams. The McGovern budget insists on no more Vietnams.

The Nixon budget gives the Pentagon everything it wants and billions more than it needs. The McGovern budget puts the excessive billions where they belong—into industries that will build and enhance life at home, rather than destroying life abroad; into our schools, our neighborhoods, our health care, and our environment.

And when this comparison becomes clear, it will not be the American people but Richard Nixon who has something to fear in this campaign.

Second, as president I would seek a fair-share tax reform to raise approximately $22 billion in additional revenue by 1975.

Let us end artificially high tax rates that are meaningless and enact a realistic rate structure that means what it says.

Let us not impose taxes in bold print and then give them back in fine print to a favored few.

Let us treat all taxpayers alike no matter how they make their living.

Let there be no more mythical tax paupers who, in fact, receive hundreds of thousands of dollars in real income but pay little or nothing in taxes.

I have said for years that the federal tax structure is unfair because it burdens the many and benefits special interests. How can anyone defend the following real-life case, taken from the U.S. Treasury's own report: This American enjoyed an income of $2,300,000 from oil and gas, capital gains, and dividends and interest; he paid tax at less than half the 14 percent rate a working person pays on the first $1,000 of taxable earnings.

Last spring, I proposed a series of changes in the tax code to make the system more equitable. Since then, Senator Mansfield and Chairman Mills have introduced legislation to review the whole range of tax credits, tax deductions, and tax breaks. I fully support that legislation because I believe that the most effective strategy now is an effort to close selected tax loopholes.

Of course, tax review without tax reform would mock its own purpose. Any fair review will reveal that we must phase out the following federal tax preferences:

—We must phase out the tax preference or loophole for capital gains, while at the same time enacting extended averaging provisions. Money made by money should be taxed at the same rate as money made by men. Tax justice demands equal treatment for Americans who earn their living with a shovel or a slide rule, and Americans who live on stock market and property gains.

—We must phase out as well the loophole for unrealized capital gains at death, with an exception for estates of reasonable size, a deferral of taxes on property left to a spouse, and, once again, extended averaging provisions. The inevitability of death should not assure the avoidability of taxes.

—We must phase out tax loopholes for the owners of oil, gas, and other natural resources. These loopholes offer compensation far greater than actual depletion would warrant. There is no allowance for the depletion of a worker's strength and years; at the least, there should not be an excessive allowance for the depletion of a corporation's mineral assets.

—We must phase out loopholes for certain kinds of real estate development, as we phase in a system of direct assistance for needed housing construction. Too often today, tax preferences that are supposed to encourage the construction of essential housing have become subsidies for luxury apartments and commercial buildings. Every family's home should provide decent shelter, but housing should not provide a tax shelter for the rich investor.

—We must also give states and municipalities a sounder option to raise revenue than tax-exempt bonds. Only 70 percent of the federal tax exemption for the interest on such bonds benefits local government; the other 30 percent benefits a well-to-do handful of bondholders. The new option should permit taxable bond issues with a federal subsidy for 50 percent of the interest costs. Then better public services for our people will not depend on a better break for the privileged.

—We must close the loophole for the farming losses of those who are not really farmers. A farmer is someone who works his fields, not someone who uses his land to bury his income where the tax collector cannot find it.

—We must at long last deal decisively with the loophole for excess investment interest. Wealthy taxpayers should no longer be able to borrow money for capital investments that do not generate taxable income, while deducting the interest on the loan from other income and thus deferring or totally escaping their just taxes.

—Finally, we must phase out corporate tax loopholes which

no longer serve a useful purpose. We should repeal the accelerated depreciation allowance of 1971 and set realistic depreciation guidelines. We should revise the investment tax credit to assure that after 1975, it will be designed to reward only increases in investment that would not otherwise be made. We should demand even-handed tax treatment for American business abroad and enterprises here at home. Corporations should be encouraged to export their products, but they should not be allowed a special tax break merely because they earn their income overseas.

In addition to the billions raised by these changes, we should strive for fairness by replacing estate and gift taxes with a single accessions tax. There should be a 100 percent exemption for the inheritance of a spouse, for moderate legacies, and for wholly-owned family enterprises. But there should also be a progressive rate structure to prevent the increasing concentration of wealth in the hands of a few. At the same time, this structure should protect the right of Americans to leave a fair share of their property to their heirs, with each generation bearing a reasonable share of the tax cost.

Now let us again compare fact with fear and the Nixon position on tax reform with the McGovern position.

The Nixon position is that we must wait until next year for specific tax proposals. The McGovern position is explicitly stated this year.

The Nixon scare tactic is that the McGovern tax reform would force Americans to pay half of their income in taxes. The fact is that my proposals would take only an extra one and a half percent of our gross national product in taxes—and no American whose income comes from wages and salaries would pay one penny more in federal taxes than he does now. Let me repeat that: No American whose income comes from wages and salaries would pay one penny more in taxes than he does now. Who would pay more? Corporations and individuals who are today exempted from paying their fair share by tax loopholes.

The Nixon position is that the allocation of resources should be determined by tax loopholes, not national needs. The McGovern position is that free enterprise and social responsibility must coexist side by side.

Finally, the Nixon position is that real tax reform would damage investment and destroy initiative. The McGovern position is that business and investors can prosper in an equitable society. I favor tax justice, not tax confiscation.

Today, the individual tax rate for the top bracket is 70 percent. That rate is a fiction, not a fact. Because the wealthy benefit so disproportionately from tax loopholes, personal income taxes do not average more than 32 percent on even the very highest incomes.

So as we phase in full taxation of capital gains, we should also phase in an effective maximum tax rate of 48 percent on both earned and unearned income. This is the same maximum rate applied to corporations today. By closing loopholes and applying that rate to wealthy individuals, we will end up with a net increase of about $22 billion in federal revenues, without decreasing the incentives for growth and initiative. That is the McGovern position. The Nixon position is at best a mystery and at worst a promise made to be broken.

And once this comparison is clear, it will not be the American people but Richard Nixon who has something to fear in 1972.

Together, the tax justice and military cutbacks I have proposed would approximate $54 billion. The total cost of additions to the national budget by a Democratic administration would be less than that. Only with new revenues and different priorities can we and would we move forward with new programs. This is the fundamental choice before the American people.

And if we make the right choice, we can fulfill an agenda that includes revenue-sharing with our cities and states and aid for rural development. It provides for better education, cleaner air and water, quality health care, and a bill of rights for Vietnam veterans and policemen. It makes possible a host of important advances, ranging from safer streets to stricter enforcement of occupational safety.

I have discussed most of this agenda in detail before. Two proposals merit special attention here today.

First, as president I would propose $15 billion to local school systems to assure substantial property tax relief.

The weight of property taxes is crushing the average home-owner in every part of the nation. At the same time, our schools are being short-changed because frustrated voters are turning down tax increases. In some cities and towns, schools have even been closed down.

We must secure a good education for our children without the insecurity of higher property taxes for their parents. The federal government should assume a third of the costs of public elementary and secondary education.

Richard Nixon also has a plan for property tax relief. It is a secret plan—which is the same kind of plan he promised for peace in Vietnam four years ago. I think that this time the secret plan is to raise taxes, not to reduce them.

I strongly believe that if Mr. Nixon is reelected—a prospect I seldom dwell upon—he will call for higher taxes in the form of a national sales tax. This Nixon sales tax would leave the loopholes wide open, but it would hit hardest the working class, the poor, the older people, and middle-income families.

To take the sting out, the President will call it a value added tax. But a sales tax by any other name smells the same.

The Nixon answer to the grievances of taxpayers is to sub-stitute one regressive tax for another.

The McGovern answer is $15 billion for quality education and property tax relief, financed by cutting military waste and securing tax justice.

When this comparison becomes clear, it will not be the American people but Richard Nixon who has something to fear in 1972.

Second, as president I would inaugurate a system of National Income Insurance as an alternative to the present welfare mess.

Richard Nixon ended the wrong war—the war on joblessness, hunger, and poverty. I believe that it is time to renew that war—which is the one a McGovern administration will wage and win.

In recent months, I have said that we must replace a welfare mess which is unfair both to those who pay for it and to those it seeks to serve. I have set forth principles for change and reform. I have discussed a number of options that seem to me consistent with those principles. After long weeks of testing, criticism, and evaluation of our present and future needs, I believe we can end the present welfare tangle in a humane and sensible way.

Jobs are the cornerstone of my policy. I will take whatever steps are necessary to guarantee a job opportunity to every man and woman in America who is able to work. I have already urged a $10 billion federal investment in new jobs through government contracts with industry.

Our highest economic priority is the lowest possible unemployment—to be achieved by vigorous action in both the public and the private sectors. I recognize that a full employment economy—which I am detemined to build—will also require a determined policy to protect the nation against inflation.

In that context, I propose today a system of National Income Insurance. Its three parts would be fully operational in 1975.

First, we should reinforce the job creation of a full employment economy by providing useful public-service jobs to as many as a million heads of household who would not otherwise earn enough to stay off welfare. This would cost $6 billion—and that cost would cover administrative expenses and wages at minimum or prevailing levels.

The best job incentive is a job opening. The best answer to welfare is work. And that is my answer. Within the next three years, by guaranteeing jobs, we can reach the point where three and a half million Americans are living on the earnings of breadwinners rather than on relief.

Second, we should expand Social Security to over three million people who would otherwise be on welfare. At a net cost of $3 billion from general revenues, Social Security would then provide complete coverage for aged, blind, and disabled Americans, and a monthly payment of at least $150. Older citizens should not be forced to turn to welfare because they are asked to settle for retirement benefits as low as $85 a month.

Guaranteed job opportunity and expanded Social Security would substantially reduce the welfare rolls. The number of Americans on welfare in 1975 would be cut by 30 percent.

Third, we should assist as generously as we can the twelve million people—largely dependent children and mothers—outside Social Security who will not be able to work in 1975. At a cost of $5 billion above current budgetary projections, we should set an annual minimum of approximately $4,000 in cash and in food stamps for a family of four with no other income. This additional money would also permit full federal financing and administration with uniform standards, lifting the burden of welfare off the backs of states and localities. It would be an indirect and urgently needed form of revenue sharing.

One of my first acts as president would be to send a message to Congress calling for immediate action on the three programs which constitute National Income Insurance—jobs for those who are able to work, a reasonable income for those who cannot work, and truly adequate Social Security.

Beyond this, we must resolve the question of income supplements for working people who, in spite of their labor, still have trouble making ends meet. Even the unacceptable Nixon Family Assistance Plan recognizes the need to boost the incomes of those who earn too little. Yet it is difficult to predict their economic future in a situation of full employment, expanded Social Security, national health insurance, property tax relief, and other advances of a McGovern administration. There seems little doubt that their position would improve substantially.

Nevertheless, I have asked some of the nation's leading economists to continue work on a system of tax credits and tax reductions to assist low- and moderate-income persons. The ultimate resolution of this question must be the subject of careful study by both the Congress and the Executive Branch.

Again, I ask you to compare fact with fear and the Nixon welfare program with the McGovern plan for National Income Insurance.

The Nixon welfare program will provide only a handful of new jobs in 1975. National Income Insurance will create almost one million jobs so that the father who has been forced during the Nixon years to support his children on welfare can once again support them with the wages of his work.

And when this comparison becomes clear, it will not be the American people but Richard Nixon who has something to fear in 1972.

But no matter what I say here today, I do not think that the President will mute his call to fear. We may still hear that my proposals will increase taxes on every family with an income above $12,000, or $15,000, or whatever level the White House invents tomorrow—but the figures prove that no family will face a tax increase if they live on earned income rather than investments.

We will still hear the incredible claim of the President's acceptance speech that new Democratic programs will cost $144 billion—but the figures show that their total cost is actually less than the total dividend from military reductions and tax reform.

And when we hear the cries of alarm and the call to fear, we may properly ask:

—What are the specific Nixon programs for the next four years?

—What will they cost and how will the money be raised?

—What Americans will receive more from their government and who will pay more in taxes?

The President has not answered these questions, while I have responded openly to similar questions about my own plans.

Indeed, this may be the first national campaign in memory where we can know with greater certainty the results of electing the challenger than of reelecting the incumbent.

I seek a budget in which the income to finance improvements balances the cost of those improvements. I seek an economy with direction instead of a directed economy. I seek to make hard choices so that we can be militarily strong, economically prosperous, and socially responsible at the same time. I seek, in short, a balanced economy.

It is difficult to know what the Republicans are seeking except four more years in the White House—and, I suspect, yet another eight years under Spiro T. Agnew.

I did not come here today with the expectation that Wall Street would rejoice at my words. But I believe that you should think twice before you vote Republican.

John Kennedy once said: "A rising tide lifts all boats." The tide of the American economy has been ebbing since 1969— just as it always has under Republican administrations. A Democratic administration will turn that tide—as Democratic presidents from Franklin Roosevelt to Lyndon Johnson did in other times. This year, you should ask yourselves whether you really prefer to be stranded on a sea of sluggish growth, with tax loopholes your only consolation—or whether you can accept both higher profits and fairer taxes. After all, even a tax loophole is no help if you have no income to be taxed.

So let us mount a rising tide to lift the boats of labor and business, the wealthy and the poor alike, to a record high. And let us recognize what is not good for business.

It is not good for business to have recurring recessions.

It is not good for business to reelect a president with no vision of our economic future.

It is not good for business to perpetuate an administration that has denied our youth an admiration for the nation's greatness.

What is good for business is a balanced economy, and a people confident of the essential decency of their leaders.

And in this case, what is good for business is essential for the country. We cannot permanently exist part in prosperity, part in poverty, and with the majority of our people under relentless economic pressure. You can explain tax loopholes to a client—but you cannot justify them to a steelworker. You cannot justify to him the fact that there are millionaires who pay no taxes at all, the fact that Standard Oil pays a lower percentage of its income in taxes than he does, the fact that the wealthy enjoy tax preferences most Americans cannot share. These facts have fueled fires of frustration and discontent across the land. And if we reject prudent tax justice now, radical tax changes may be forced upon us later. We would do well to heed the warning of a decade ago: "If a free society will not help the many who are poor, it cannot save the few who are rich."

Yet this is not just a matter of self-interest or necessity. Above all, it is a matter of moral right.

How can any of us rest easy when we know that, as we meet here, there are children in this city who are without food, thousands who are ill and without care, aged men and women who are without hope, and workers who toil in danger and filth for little reward? Our government is the expression of our national conscience. It is time to look into that conscience and to prove by the way we govern that we really do believe in what we celebrate as our way of life. It is time to recall that the promise of America was not a pledge to the privileged, but a covenant with all our people. Let us keep that covenant now.

In his acceptance speech, Richard Nixon charged that the Democratic Party was intent on tearing down America's great building of economic wealth and might. But our real complaint is that the building has become an insecure palace for the wealthy, with too little room for the rest of our citizens. And our real aim, in the words of Franklin Roosevelt, is "to restore that temple to the ancient truths." The building which is our society cannot be preserved by those who live in it without repairing it, but only by those who perfect the foundations and strengthen the structure to stand for another two hundred years.

This is the cause of the Democratic Party in 1972.

I do not know if I have made any converts to that cause today.

But you can be assured that as the son of a poor clergyman from South Dakota, I treasure the opportunities America has opened to me. I loved this country as a combat bomber pilot in World War Two. I love it all the more today. I believe the greatness of America lies in its capacity to renew itself by reasserting from time to time those enduring ideals of human dignity and brotherhood with which we began. I find those ideals fully compatible with good jobs for our workers, good services for our people, compassion for the poor, the old, and the afflicted —and solid, socially useful investment opportunity for our business community.

The marriage of social responsibility and an enlightened government has always been good for business and for the nation. It is the foundation that will enable us to sing again, with new pride:

"This land is your land, this land is my land.

"From California to the New York Island,

"From the redwood forests to the Gulf Stream waters,

"This land was made for you and me."

Four Years and No Prosperity

In all I delivered five "fireside chats" during the course of the 1972 campaign. They were an attempt to reach voters in large numbers and to focus the campaign on the truly critical issues. Obviously they did not accomplish as much as we hoped. It would have been wiser to begin them earlier, perhaps in August, as a counter to the public concern raised by our vice-presidential woes.

But if they did not convert large numbers of voters, these speeches did elicit the greatest financial response from ordinary citizens of any political broadcasts in history. They paid for themselves and much more besides. And I also believe they were then and continue to be now among the clearest statements of what was at stake in 1972.

The televised speech on economic issues was by far the most difficult to prepare. We could envision sets being switched off in millions of homes across the country if I launched into a dry statistical dissertation. So I left the more academic approach for other forums, and spoke to the personal stake we all have in how government manages the economy.

Television Address

OCTOBER 20, 1972

Ten days ago I asked you to think about an issue that challenges the conscience of us all—whether we will have four more years of war in Vietnam, or at long last restore this country to peace.

I asked you to judge this election according to a standard described by Mr. Nixon himself on October 9, 1968, and I quote: "Those who have had a chance for four years and could not produce peace should not be given another chance."

Tonight, I ask you to think about a different but related issue where I have equally strong feelings and where you have a great stake—whether we will have four more years of unemployment, unfair taxes, and a rising cost of living, or a new period of prosperity for all our people. I ask you to judge the Nixon Administration on this issue by the same test you should apply to their record on Vietnam: Those who have had a chance for four years and could not produce prosperity should not be given another chance.

Tonight, as I speak to you, at least two million Americans are out of work who were hard at work four years ago.

The Nixon Administration has given us the highest inflation in two decades. Tonight the dollar you saved four years ago is worth 82 cents.

The Nixon Administration has given us the highest budget deficits in three decades. Tonight the $80 billion deficit piled up in the last four years accounts for one-fifth of the entire national debt accumulated ever since the days of George Washington.

And the Nixon Administration has given us a deficit in our international trade for the first time in the twentieth century. Tonight skilled hands in our country are idle because we have exported our jobs instead of our products, and the dollar, once the strongest currency on earth, has been devalued for the first time in four decades.

Now, these are the cold, hard facts of the Nixon economic failure. But behind every statistic there is a tale of human tragedy. A father must let his life insurance lapse because he has no job. A farmer is driven off the land his family has tilled for generations. A factory closes and a town dies. Prices rise and your standard of life goes down. And it is a time of lost dreams, of homes not bought because they are suddenly too expensive, the interest rates are too high, and the property tax is too heavy. It is a time of sons and daughters not sent to college, and it is a time when older Americans have even less than the too little they had before.

What has gone wrong? Every single time this administration has faced an important economic choice, they have picked a policy that is right for the few and wrong for you.

Inflation was a problem when Mr. Nixon was elected, but his solutions made it worse and created new problems besides. He could have followed the example of John Kennedy, who invoked the prestige and power of the presidency during the steel crisis to prevent an excessive price increase. Instead, Mr. Nixon chose a course that robbed you to reward the rich.

His administration raised interest rates. Now, that helped the investors and the bankers who loan the money and collect the interest, but what did it mean to the average family? If you buy a modest $15,000 home under the Nixon Administration, you have to pay an extra $8,100 in interest on a standard mortgage. That is $8,100 more than the same home cost when the Democrats left office. And now a Nixon commission has proposed removing consumer protection by permitting unlimited interest rates on the things you buy. The sky will be the limit.

The second Nixon answer to inflation was higher unemployment, and that was a deliberate decision. The White House thought that if more of you were out of work you would have less to spend, and if you spent less, demand would fall and so would prices. They were wrong. Their policy did not work.

And they were wrong in a deeper sense because they forgot that the first obligation of government is to you. No president has the right to destroy your livelihood for the sake of an economic game plan. How little they must care about you if they think of you, not as people who have a right to earn a living, but as numbers to be unemployed at will. And how much they must care for the special interests if they are ready to force two million workers out of work, but reluctant to even touch the prices and profits of the privileged.

Finally, as an election year approached, the Administration seemed to change course. They announced a new program of wage and price controls, and they struck a bargain with you: If you kept your wages down, they would hold prices down. That promise has been broken. Once again the Administration has done what was right for the few and wrong for you. They have dictated wages, but they have defaulted on prices.

The major preoccupation of the Nixon Price Commission has been to protect corporations, not to prevent inflation. The Commission has approved nine-tenths of all requests for price increases almost as a matter of course. In a single three-month period they rubber-stamped one hundred rate-increase applications for gas, electric, and telephone companies at a cost to you of $2 billion.

So, what the Administration has given us is price controls that are unfair, unenforced, and unsuccessful. Prices have gone up 30 percent faster under the Nixon controls than the Nixon Administration promised. Inflation is worse than what it was when they started. Indeed, your dollar has lost more value in the last four years than in the eight years of President Kennedy and President Johnson combined.

A week ago someone sent me a letter with copies of two grocery ads in the Boston *Globe,* one from January 19, 1969, the day before Mr. Nixon was inaugurated, and the other from October 5, 1972. In the '69 ad round steak was 94 cents a pound; in the 1972 ad it was $1.45. In the 1969 ad bread cost 25 cents a loaf; now it costs 34 cents. Bacon is up from 69 cents a pound to 89 cents. A ten-ounce jar of coffee is up from 99 cents to $1.37.

In 1968, candidate Nixon promised us that we would not have to choose between unemployment and inflation. Now he has made many promises, but this one he kept. He has given us both unemployment and inflation. The result is that $80 billion Nixon deficit which has massively increased the national debt.

Now, what does this mean to you? Just the interest on that debt will take $100 a year from every American family. Not just this year, but every year from now on. You bear the cost of that. Someday so will your children and your grandchildren after them.

And how will that cost be carried? Like all costs of government it will be carried more and more by ordinary Americans through a tax system that helps the rich and hurts the man in the middle. For on taxes too this administration comforts the wealthy few and afflicts those who can just barely get by. They cut corporate taxes last year by $8 billion, but there was no tax cut for you, and a tax system that was already unfair is now a moral outrage.

In a recent year, the five largest steel companies cleared $380 million. What do you think they paid in federal taxes? Not a single dime. Who made up the difference? You did. You paid your taxes and the taxes of the steel companies too.

Last spring in Kenosha, Wisconsin, I met an eighty-two-year-old widow who was living out her life on $145 a month. She owned her own little home. She and her husband had bought it a generation ago, but property taxes now take one-third of her entire annual income. She did not know how much longer she could hold on. She asked me why the country has forgotten her after she has given a lifetime to the country.

The difference between her and the steel companies says it all. Our tax system mocks our most precious ideals of fairness and justice. It divides Americans into two classes—those who pay more than is right and those who pay less than they should.

Mr. Nixon disagrees, and that is a fundamental difference between us. He opposed real tax reform in 1969. I supported it. He fought for a larger oil depletion allowance than we now have. I fought against it. He has opened more loopholes in the tax code. I have worked to close the loopholes.

Now the Nixon Administration seeks to blind you to their failures and their favoritism by scaring you about me. They know who you will support if issues like tax reform and jobs and inflation are honestly debated. They know your true interests are with the Democratic Party in 1972, but they do not want you to know. So they are trying to frighten you into voting against yourselves. They are trying to trick you into thinking that I would damage your economic security even more than they already have.

There is too little time tonight to answer the torrent of distortion that has poured forth from the Nixon campaign. Instead, let us discuss what is perhaps the most glaring single falsehood of all. You have probably seen Mr. Nixon's television commercial which shows a construction worker looking down from a skyscraper on a crowd of people, all of them supposedly on relief. The commercial claims that I plan to put half the country on welfare, and it asks: "Who will pay the bill?

Now, the public-relations men who produced that commercial and the candidate who is putting it on the air know it is a lie. It is true that in my search for a way out of the welfare mess I once discussed a plan—a plan by some of the nation's leading economists—for a $1,000 grant to every citizen that would be taxed back from those who do not need it. But it is also true, and it is a matter of public record, that I have rejected this idea, just as Mr. Nixon advocated and then rejected a similar guaranteed-income plan. Attacking me for it now makes no more sense than attacking Mr. Nixon for it, or attacking him for taking a hard line toward Communist China, which was exactly his position until he changed his mind and went to Peking.

A leader who will not change his mind on the basis of new facts or new insight is no leader at all; he is a disaster. The critical question is whether he has improved his policy or betrayed his principles, and I have consistently held to the principle that we must replace a welfare system that is unfair, both to those who pay for it and to those it seeks to serve.

For those who are too old, or too young, or too weak to work, we must ensure a minimum standard of life. But no one who can work should be on welfare. I have proposed a program for jobs that would help cut the number of Americans on welfare by 30 percent in 1975.

Now, Mr. Nixon also says he favors payrolls over welfare rolls, and he talks about the work ethic. But he has done more than any other president in recent history to reinforce the welfare ethic. In the four years of the Nixon Administration six million Americans have been added to welfare at a cost to the taxpayers of $5 billion.

The difference between Mr. Nixon and me is that he has raised welfare to a record high, while I have an open and specific plan to reduce it and to put this nation back to work.

This is the first of three steps I would take as president to give your government back to you and to secure a fair prosperity for all Americans.

First, I would ask Congress to enact the necessary legislation to guarantee a job opportunity for every man and woman in this country who is able to work.

My highest economic priority is the lowest possible unemployment. This would be achieved through federal action:

—To stimulate demand and open up jobs in the private sector;

—To contract with industry for housing, for public transportation, for water and sewer systems, and other things we urgently need;

—And to underwrite jobs in state and local government for the unemployed.

This program calls for an immediate $10 billion investment in new jobs, and it would invest an additional $6 billion each year in jobs for people who would otherwise be on welfare.

Republican politicians say that we cannot reach full employment with the cuts I would make in military waste. Now, they are right that I intend to end that waste, no matter what that does to the insatiable appetites of those who profit from war and rumors of war. But they are wrong when they say this will cause unemployment. In fact, it will create more employment. We do not need to send our sons to war in order to put their parents back to work. The same amount of money that will provide one million jobs building missiles and bombs will generate one and a half million jobs in peaceful pursuits. And I have offered this pledge: No job that depends on the defense budget will be eliminated until there is a comparable civilian job to replace it.

I want this nation to be militarily strong, but I also want us to heed General Eisenhower's warning that if the military takes too much, it actually weakens the nation.

Second, I would adopt a tough, even-handed system to curb the cost of living. I would use the moral and legal authority of the presidency to prevent excessive price and wage increases. By law, the present controls will end next April. Before that, I would ask the Congress for power to suspend or to roll back any inflationary price or wage decision in a major industry. And I would not hesitate to exercise that power if persuasion and pressure fail.

Of course, any system to stop inflation is only as good as the people who direct it. If an administration is biased toward big business, as this administration is, the system will be both ineffective and unfair. Already there are reports that the White House is ready to impose stricter wage controls after the election. That means that you will have even less purchasing power, while prices continue to climb.

So the real question is this: Whom do you trust to give equal treatment to both wages and prices? Mr. Nixon's campaign is bankrolled by those who are so rich that they can give millions to elect a president who will help them get even richer. And they will ask him for more special favors. In contrast, my campaign is financed by people like you who seek nothing but an equal break for us all.

Third, I would fight to reduce the tax burden on you and to require every citizen and corporation to pay a fair share. Even though Mr. Nixon denies it during this election campaign, new revenues will be needed in the next administration. Mr. Nixon would raise them by taking more from you with a proposed national sales tax. But in my administration no one whose income comes from wages or salaries would pay one penny more in taxes, and that includes most Americans.

Instead I would close $22 billion in loopholes. Who would pay more? The corporations and the wealthy individuals who today escape through those loopholes. And you would pay less, because I would also propose a $15 billion program to reduce the property tax load by approximately one-third.

I do not want to soak the rich, but I want them to pay their fair share, and I want the government to stop piling new taxes on rank-and-file taxpayers. Mr. Nixon thinks that it is right to have a depletion allowance for oil, but no allowance for the depletion of a worker's back. Mr. Nixon thinks that it is right to have higher taxes for Americans who earn their living by hard work and lower taxes for those who live on stock market and property gains. I think that money earned by money should be taxed at the same rate as money earned by man.

Now, closing tax loopholes and reducing military waste will cover the cost of property tax reduction and the new programs that I have proposed. And if you hear politicians advocating more military spending and bigger programs but no new taxes, then you can be certain they are trying to deceive you.

Let's face it: This election is more than a contest between George McGovern and Richard Nixon. It is a fundamental struggle between the little people of America and the big rich of America, between the average working man or woman and a powerful elite.

The special interests have given Mr. Nixon a $40 million campaign fund. They know that I mean what I say and they don't like it, and they are trying to stop me.

The Nixon public-relations experts are very clever. They are using every technique in the book to persuade you that the Administration is acting in your best interests. But how many of you can really say that your life has improved in the last four years? How many of you can say that your city streets are safer, your tax burdens fairer, your grocery bills lower, or your sense of security and well-being stronger? Do you really want four more years of these policies?

I believe we can do better. I believe we can achieve Woodrow Wilson's vision of a nation that belongs not to the politicians or the privileged, but to the people who labor all day and go home tired in the evening. I believe that we can restore a leadership that stands for you, not against you, a government that is not for sale to anyone because it is fair to everyone.

Let me end on a personal note. I was born in a small Wesleyan Methodist parsonage in Avon, South Dakota. My parents were not rich, but they were thrifty and they worked hard. They instilled in me the importance of those values. I think that good businessmen, good farmers, and good workers deserve good earnings and fair taxes.

After going off to war as a pilot in 1943, I returned to finish my education. My wife Eleanor and I both worked while we reared our children and while I studied at Northwestern University.

Later, we took on the task of trying to build a healthy, two-party system in our home state of South Dakota—and that was hard work. It was hard work to be elected to the United States Senate. And it is hard work to run for the presidency of the United States as an underdog, underfinanced, and opposed by the unprecedented millions of dollars that the special interests have poured into Mr. Nixon's campaign.

But I like hard work, and I love this nation. America has been good to me and I want to be the kind of president who will see to it that America is good to every one of her people. I want us to claim the promise of Isaiah: "The people shall be righteous and they shall inherit the land."

DIRECTIONS

A campaign which does not take specific positions on the issues fails the American people, even if it succeeds in winning their votes. But a campaign which offers nothing more than specific positions also falls short. For a candidate's programs should be more than a collection of proposed actions; they should be an expression of basic purposes as well. From the beginning I sought to articulate the larger aims of the campaign in many contexts. To a college audience, like the students at Hunter, I spoke of the war, of frustration in the face of it and over the unresponsiveness of the American system, and of the need to shape more open political and public institutions. In St. Louis,

I spoke at one time for a more decent vision of this land and at another time of a more democratic presidency. In Minneapolis, at a political rally, I spoke not only of the obvious issues, but of the less obvious yet enduring differences between our great political parties.

So, although they sometimes suggest the destinations of policy, the speeches in this section emphasize a direction for leadership and action. We not only wanted to "get this country moving again"; we wanted to move it once again in the right direction.

The South: "The Eyes of America Are Upon You"

In December of 1970, I went to Texas for a rally to help pay off the debt Ralph Yarborough had accumulated in a losing race for reelection to the Senate. That event, honoring a statesman who had struggled against discrimination throughout his political life, seemed the right time to make some observations about Mr. Nixon's "Southern Strategy," and to begin a search for the better instincts of the South.

Ralph Yarborough Appreciation Dinner

AUSTIN, TEXAS | DECEMBER 15, 1970

May I follow Bernard Rappaport's eloquent introduction by thanking the people of Texas who brought us together as friends of two beautiful people—Ralph and Opal Yarborough.

It is an honor to share this special occasion with an old and dear friend—the brand new senator from Minnesota, Hubert Humphrey. Let me tell you that the launching of my political career in hidebound Republican South Dakota in the 1950's would not have been possible without the help and inspiration of Hubert Humphrey.

And I'm proud, too, to share this stage with a great governor, and now a courageous senator, Harold Hughes of Iowa.

Texas is rich in emotion for all Democrats.

It was in Texas that John F. Kennedy first faced down the issue of religious prejudice when ten years ago he won the confidence of the Protestant clergy at Houston and then the hearts of the Texas voters.

And it is Texas that has given the nation a long train of leaders, including the late Speaker Rayburn and President Johnson.

So we meet in a historic place filled with memories for the entire nation.

This celebration must seem strange to some. For we celebrate in honor of one who has suffered a political defeat.

But we celebrate something beyond the counting of votes.

We celebrate the courage of a statesman with peace in his soul—and steel in his spine.

The strength of a nation is in its vision and its faith. Ralph Yarborough is one of those rare men who reminds America of her greatness. He has held the vision and kept the faith.

This is a party gathering, but I do not come as a party man. A wide variety of convictions are represented here, but I do not bring a message of reconciliation. We share many goals, but I do not come in the name of tranquil unity. Rather I come here —to Texas, a state founded in rebellion—in hopes that you will lead the South in resistance and struggle—resistance and struggle against that conspiracy between a few Northern interests and some Southern leaders to divide the South from the nation, stifle its growth, and deny its people a full share in the abundance of America. And I also come on a most important search —to see if your growing self-confidence will make it possible for the South, once again, to help sustain the American spirit.

For if you can solve your own problems, you can help the rest of us to solve ours. The South, more strongly than any section, clings to a belief which values men more than their goods or bank accounts, which labors to preserve the bonds of community and family and place which tie men to their fellows. And these beliefs now represent the common hunger of all America.

Our country is confused, uneasy, and often in turmoil. Its people are searching for a way of life that will give each man a sense of belonging, of sharing in some great purpose.

Thus, if you are able to unshackle yourself from today's injustice and from distorted memories, the South—with Texas at the helm—can shape the American future just as it molded the American past.

The first step is to expose and reject that corrupt fraud which calls itself a Southern Strategy. The words are modern, but the strategy is old. It began during Reconstruction and, except for brief periods, has scarred an entire century.

What is this Southern Strategy? It is not very complicated. When you ask about education for your children, it replies: Fear the black man. When you seek peace abroad and reasoned discourse at home, it replies: Fear the young. When you demand jobs and expanding opportunity, it replies: Fear the poor. When you ask why the South should lag behind the economy of the country, why there should be more poverty here and most of it white, it replies: We shall appoint a Carswell or a Connally to show how we love you.

What is this Southern Strategy? It is this. It says to the South: Let the poor stay poor, let your economy trail the nation, forget about decent homes and medical care for all your people, choose officials who will oppose every effort to benefit the many at the expense of the few—and in return, we will try to overlook the rights of the black man, appoint a few Southerners to high office, and lift your spirits by attacking "the Eastern establishment" whose bank accounts we are filling with your labor and your industry. It is a clever strategy. But it is not for the benefit of the people of the South. And it is not for the benefit of the American nation.

They truly seem to believe you can be persuaded to trade in your hopes for the future, your rightful share in the American destiny—in return for slogans, a few appointments, and the illusion that the black man can be permanently suppressed. I think they are in for an awakening. Those city slickers from Whittier and Baltimore are going to learn that no one out-trades a Texan. And with your leadership, their Southern Strategy will prove to be a strategy for defeat in the South.

Your best leadership is more crucial today than ever. For the era of Northern liberalism is drawing to an end. It was a great period. But it is gone. It was right to fight for higher standards of living, for greater income. And for those who are still poor, that remains a deeply moral goal.

But we have also found that the pursuit of wealth and power is a dead end. Citizens of all ages are groping for new values—or rather they look for restoration of old values in the modern context. I believe they can find them in the South.

For there are elements of Southern life which can liberate the nation of today, just as the great Southerners of two centuries ago helped to liberate the colonies—not just politically, but in spirit—from the oppressions of the old world.

There remains here a belief that life is more than the accumulation of material goods; that the individual is not just a solitary wanderer, but a person whose place in a community and family is to be secured and respected.

There is here the unyielding desire that individuals be allowed to shape their own lives and destinies, and not be guided and controlled by giant bureaucracies or huge and impersonal institutions.

Most of all, there is a sense of America—not just as a place, a piece of geography, not as a storehouse of wealth and arms, but as an idea and a spirit, as a country with a great and noble purpose: to do justice to its own people and to illuminate the road to freedom for the suffering and oppressed of all lands. It is a sense of America—not as the destroyer, not as the fearful giant lashing out to protect itself, but as the city on the hill, the friend of the weak, the hope of all mankind—not because we are rich and powerful, but because we are free and just, and because we wish others to live as they would live, and not as we command.

That is the core of patriotism, and here, in Texas, that true spirit of patriotism endures and can be spread to a nation hungry to renew its belief in itself. Some carry the slogan: "America, love it or leave it." We shall reply: "We will change it so we may love it the more."

This must be our course—as Americans and as Democrats. Of course, we want to win elections, but the victory must be for something—and about something. More important than victory is our responsibility to give the people of this country a liberating and constructive alternative—to lay bare the profound malfunctions of the society, to discuss solutions that may be painful. In the rush to the center, we must not be so busy making space on either side that we fail to notice the dead end ahead.

If we Democrats reflect the fears of people rather than their hopes, seek security from weakness rather than risk confidence in the moral decency of our citizens, then we will deserve to lose. And we will lose. For no matter how fast we follow that path, the Republicans will always be around the next corner.

But if we do begin to change and restore America, I believe the guiding impulse will come from this section of the country —from Texas and the South. Walt Whitman wrote: "The Northern ice and rain that began me nourished me to the end, but the hot sun of the South is to fully ripen my songs." If you can liberate yourselves from the old stereotypes and illusions, the deceits and injustices, then the Southern seedbed of our democracy will also fulfill the mature republic.

There can be no more noble opportunity and no greater burden. Keep up the battle. America's future may depend on the outcome.

> The eyes of America are upon you
> All the livelong day;
> The eyes of America are upon you
> And they will not go away.

The Young Can
Make the System Work

Although the McGovern campaign gathered strength from citizens of all ages and a broad variety of groups, it was from the outset a youthful exercise—staffed, managed, and in many ways inspired by young first voters and young adults. In 1970 and 1971, I spoke at scores of college campuses .and took every chance to meet with young voters who were not in school. Even then the pace was grueling (in fact, my small advance and scheduling team took one line out of this speech—"I seek no purposeless test of physical endurance"—and pinned it up on the wall as a message to *them*). But these encounters with young Americans were a constant source of hope, even of confidence, that we could win. Throughout the primaries and state conventions, our youthful strategists were better than the most highly seasoned old pros.

Hunter College

NEW YORK CITY | DECEMBER 9, 1971

In January of this year I announced that I am a candidate for the presidency of the United States.

Let me tell you just briefly why I did that.

Since 1963, as a senator, I have been speaking out against, and proposing steps to end, a war in Indochina that still goes on today. I have felt every bit of the frustration that goes with seeing my country involved in a disastrous foreign adventure that is still with us eight years later—still wasting our youth and our treasure, still inflicting merciless punishment on helpless Asians, still identifying America with a dictator in Saigon who defiles everything this country stands for.

The president of the United States can end that foul war with a stroke of the pen, and I want to do just that.

For just as long, as a senator, I have been searching for means of converting from a war to a peace economy—to stop the hopeless and senseless competition in superfluous arms, and to put people to work on the new houses and schools and hospitals and transportation systems we need so desperately here at home. And those efforts have been frustrated, too, as the arms industries and the military, with the help of successive presidents, have won nearly every battle.

The president of the United States can reverse that situation, and that is what I want to do.

As a senator, and as chairman of the Select Committee on Nutrition and Human Needs, I have been outraged by the mental, physical, and emotional destruction of millions of our people by poverty and hunger. And I have seen our proposals to end those appalling conditions fail because the Executive Branch cuts the funds.

The president of the United States can find those funds and apply them, and that is what I plan to do.

As a senator I have seen a tax system that favors the rich over the poor; I have seen economic policies which place wealth and power in the hands of the few at the expense of the many. I have seen the minority of Americans who are red, black, and brown—and the majority who are women—kept in their excluded place by discrimination both in and out of government.

The president of the United States can change that situation, and that is what I plan to do.

I have witnessed, as a senator, the establishment of deception as accepted political strategy. I have seen leaders who find their principles in public-opinion polls and who build their political careers on prejudice and fear by playing to the worst elements in the American character.

The president of the United States can restore respect for truth. He can renew this country's commitment to justice, and he can find the compassion and decency that also live in each American. And that is the search I want to make.

Those are some of the reasons why I have undertaken this campaign—because it can make a difference who is president—because who is president can make more difference than anything else.

I have no interest in fruitless intellectual exercise.

I seek no purposeless test of physical endurance.

This is no empty gesture against the establishment.

This campaign continues a long, difficult, and determined effort to change America's direction, and I mean to see it succeed.

Our land today faces perplexing problems and overwhelming public needs. But there may be a tendency to regard them as more complicated than they are. There is a risk that some fundamental questions will be deliberated long past the time of decision.

We did not need four years of debate to decide that the Indochina war was wrong—and then another year or more to decide that it was safe to say that in public.

We do not need a blue-ribbon task force to figure out that the healthy, strong economies of Europe can afford to shoulder a bigger share of their own defense, and that U.S. troop levels there should be cut at least in half.

We do not need a study commission to determine that it is no more than empty sloganeering to talk about rearranging national priorities unless we are willing to cut that swollen military budget by at least one-third, and to start applying those funds to the domestic programs which today have a great deal more to do with both our greatness and our safety.

We need no advisory group to uncover the injustice in excluding any American from any job, from any educational opportunity, or from any office on the basis of race.

These are questions which bear on the underlying philosophy and purpose of national government in this country. And they are difficult only if they are approached in the context of the old consensus politics which attempts to feed every special interest, and to reflect every old discredited point of view, at the same time as it professes the public good.

Well, I think we have had enough of that kind of politics in this last painful decade. The promise of America will not be salvaged by those who propose to subtract a little here, add a little there, and try to be a little more decent. We have to be willing to make somebody mad, and to take some political risks, if we are to reclaim our society.

I do not hesitate to say that I stake my hopes in 1972 in large part on the energy, the wisdom, and the conscience of young Americans—on the working youth, the college and university students, and the young adults who together make up some twenty-five million first-time voters in this next election.

It has been among those people that many of our most persistent national ills have received the most relentless attention in recent years; that injustice and hypocrisy have been most often exposed; that the search for peace has been nourished until it has grown into an overwhelming national demand.

I am here today because I think you, too, have had enough of frustration. And I seek your support in the conviction that you, too, want to win the battles that have been taxing your energies, to such marginal effect, for so many painful months.

Those efforts have brought home some hard political realities.

It has become clear that those who wave Vietcong flags cannot end the war; they only cripple and confuse the quest for peace.

We have seen that those who throw epithets and stones at the police have no part to play in the search for justice; they can only offend the sense of decency upon which that search must be based.

But we have also seen that young political activists have enormous political power.

The persuading and organizing of a few thousand young workers in New Hampshire gave us the opportunity to read Lyndon Johnson's memoirs four years ahead of schedule. And the nationwide pre-convention campaign brought the peace issue before the American people as never before.

Four years later we can achieve more than a hollow negative victory.

The Commission on Democratic party reform which I chaired has written new rules of delegate selection which guarantee that the Democratic Convention next year will be the most open and the most responsive convention in our national history. Among those binding guidelines is a requirement that young voters be represented in reasonable proportion to their numbers in state delegations, and that they have the right to full participation in choosing the candidate and in writing the platform.

In 1968 America's youth was represented on the streets and in the parks of Chicago. In 1972 you will be heard in the caucuses and on the convention floor.

Also since 1968, the Twenty-sixth Amendment has extended the right to vote down to eighteen years of age. If the establishment politician had to fear your organizational muscle in the last contest, they must feel the impact of your votes as well in 1972. And if you doubt that those votes can have a decisive effect on the primaries, just consider that there will be more people eligible to vote for the first time in 1972 than there were total votes cast, on all sides, in all primaries of both parties, in 1968.

These changes do not guarantee a different result. The system has been improved since 1968, but it is only an improvement in political opportunity. The system does not work—it has to be worked, and that work has to start now.

We need to find and register and invite the participation of the people of all races and ages who have suffered the worst abuses the country has had to offer, with a campaign that can, at last, have a real effect on their lives.

Along with the most glaring injustices, we need to address those which are less obvious but which still impose constant frustration on the majority of the American people—the collapse of public services in major cities, the isolation and despair of the elderly, the shattered hopes and real fears of those who walk between the upper edge of poverty and the lower fringes of comfort.

President Nixon bases his hopes on what he calls a "silent majority" of Americans, and he defines them in demeaning and hopeless terms.

I think we can build a different majority.

It is not a majority that will welcome, or even tolerate, the bombing and burning of helpless Asians so long as the cost is reduced. It is not a majority so unthinking that it can be led around by rhetoric, or so uncaring that it can be divided on matters of style from its common interest in matters of substance.

Instead, it can be constructed from small businessmen who know that appointing William Rehnquist, having the FBI investigate Daniel Schorr, or locking up youthful pot-smokers, does nothing about the heroin enslavement that accounts for a major share of robberies, about the proliferation of handguns that has made us all fear for our lives, or about the other real causes of crime in this country.

The new majority can be found among family farmers who know that having an agricultural exhibition at the White House is not going to rescue them from a vertically integrated corporate takeover of agriculture.

It can be constructed of working men and women who see

that their best hope for progress lies not in fighting off the legitimate demands of minorities, but in building a scale of public priorities which will guarantee a job for everyone who wants to work.

It can be made up of people at every level who are fed up with government that will not respond, with government which seems to exist to serve its own convenience instead of that of the American people, with government which is almost entirely the same year in and year out, election in and election out, regardless of who is at the top.

In spite of its pain and despair—in fact because of those afflictions—the past decade can be seen among the most hopeful times in American history.

The civil-rights confrontations of the early sixties awakened the American soul to the tragedy of discrimination. They inspired the beginnings of a response to the hundred-year-old demand for equality.

But the bright promise of true equality has faltered at the higher threshold of economic justice, and the original outrage persists.

The senseless assassination and waste of great and compassionate leaders has left gaping wounds. And those bitter events also left behind a new introspection, a new willingness to search our own nature, to concern ourselves with what kind of people we are, to resolve against violence and hate.

Yet no one can say that our politics today is much improved, that we have moved to a higher standard of tolerance and respect.

The accumulation of domestic problems to crisis levels during the sixties brought with it a new sense of national responsibility for addressing human concerns and for meeting human needs. The old institutional barriers against decisive national action finally began to appear less significant than finding ways to move people from place to place, to provide enough housing, to stop the destruction of air and water, to assure equal educational opportunities, and to provide basic public services.

But those needs remain largely unmet, and those concerns unaddressed, because the resources cannot be found.

In the past decade the wrenching experience of Vietnam has brought a new examination of the ways in which, and the reasons for which, this nation goes to war. It has laid the foundation for a new understanding of the limits on American rights and responsibilities in the world, and a new awareness of the brutality and the futility of attempting to kill ideas and ideals with guns.

Yet the war is not over, and many still seem to see it as an inexplicable exception to the normal course of events, as a good cause somehow gone bad. And we still build military postures and strategies designed for no purpose other than to repeat it.

I suggest to you today that the lessons of the 1960's were purchased at too great a cost to be abandoned.

And I suggest further that those lessons have penetrated much more deeply than many suppose into the American conscience.

They wait there to be awakened by political workers who are concerned enough with change to be out now ringing doorbells, to be talking with people in their homes, and to be discussing the choices we face in 1972.

And they wait there to be inspired by leaders who have enough respect for the American people to approach them on the basis of understanding instead of doubt, truth instead of prejudice, and hope instead of fear.

That is what I propose to do.

Come help me try.

The Message They Sent

On the night of the Florida primary I made no response except to concede that Governor Wallace had won a solid victory and to caution against writing it off as racism. Then we took some time to analyze what that vote meant. And we concluded that many of the Wallace supporters were alienated from a political system that no longer responded to the genuine concerns of ordinary citizens. Responding to these concerns need not mean compromising any position. On the contrary, it called for more emphasis on the central theme we had been developing from the beginning —that government must listen once again to the people.

MILWAUKEE, WISCONSIN | MARCH 23, 1972

The night of the vote in the Florida primary there was a strong and mixed reaction to the large vote compiled by Mr. Wallace, the governor of Alabama.

Some of the candidates simply ignored the Governor's large vote—I believe that was a mistake.

Other candidates attacked the Governor and all those who voted for him as simply being for racism.

That was a mistake.

I believe the Governor is an extremist. But I believe many of the people who supported the Governor did so because they are deeply frustrated and disgusted with the way their government is ignoring their concerns and interests.

The Governor convinced those people that he cared more about their problems than any other candidate—and those concerns ranged beyond bussing to issues such as taxes, personal safety on the streets, and schools that get steadily worse.

I am not here to lecture Wallace supporters for prejudices that some have attributed to them—it is not prejudice to fear for your family's safety or to resent tax inequities. These concerns are as deeply felt in the black community as in the white.

Every poll taken in black communities has showed that more police protection is at the top of the list of concerns.

It is time to recognize this and to stop labeling people "racist" or "militant," to stop putting people in different camps, to stop inciting one American against another.

It is time to stop talking of divisiveness and to start dealing with the very real consensus that exists around these very human concerns that are felt in all our communities.

After the Governor's victory, I said I thought it would be a mistake to simply dismiss it as a racist result; I said that the Democratic candidates had better carefully consider the meaning of the Governor's victory—and respond to it in a meaningful way.

As yet, other candidates are either continuing to ignore the meaning of the Governor's vote in Florida—continuing to dismiss it as a regional racist result with, hopefully, less meaning for the rest of the country—or actually jumping on what they think is the Wallace bandwagon.

The President jumped on with his speech the other night—and Senator Hubert Humphrey jumped on with his response to the President. Senator Humphrey said: "At long last the President has been able to get his finger up in the air and sense what's going on and has decided that he would say amen to some of the things that some of the rest of us have been trying to do. He's in agreement with me. Let's get the cart where it belongs."

And that was a mistake.

Since Florida, I have given more and more thought to what the results there meant. Tonight, I am going to try and respond in a meaningful way to what the voters of Florida were telling the Democratic Party—and the country.

First, a lot of the people voted for the Governor not because they want him to be president—but because he was a tool they could use to express their anger.

If that vote had actually been for president, I think the result would have been very different.

Voters in this country are smart enough to know that the Governor is not a big enough man to govern this entire nation and its affairs with other nations.

But they are also smart enough to recognize a way of delivering a message—to use the Governor's own words—to the other candidates, and to the man who will be the nominee of the Democratic Party.

And the message they delivered was pretty clear.

They are fed up with the same old Washington politicians giving them a lot of talk about what needs to be changed in the country and then, once they get elected, changing nothing at all.

They are fed up with being told that the war is going to end and never seeing an end to the war.

They are fed up with being told that the economy is going to pick up and unemployment is going to go down—and never seeing either of those things happen.

They are fed up with being told that inflation is going to stop and prices are going down—and every time they shop for groceries, prices are higher this week than last.

They are fed up with being told that their taxes are not going to go up any more—and seeing their taxes raised while their take-home pay drops.

They are fed up with being told that their neighborhoods are going to be safe and clean—and seeing the city become more unsafe than ever before.

In short, they are fed up with being ignored by politicians who keep asking for money to solve problems that never get solved.

They are fed up—and they are mad.

And that is what the Wallace vote meant.

It was not just a vote to stop the buses.

It was not simply a vote for racism in America.

It was an angry cry from the guts of ordinary Americans against a system which doesn't seem to give a damn about what is really bothering people in this country today.

It was a vote to stop the whole damn Democratic Party and make it listen to the people for a change—instead of just to political strategists.

During the past year, my travels have forced me to spend less time at my desk and more time with people in all parts of the country. It has been a tough, bone-tiring experience. But I have come to the conviction that this crazy-quilt pattern we use to select presidential nominees is a good one because it has both tested me and opened my eyes to a world I saw only dimly in recent years.

I have walked through the stench of the paper factories and the steady noise of the shoe factories of New Hampshire—not just smiling and handing out buttons, but stopping to listen.

I have gone down into the coal mines of West Virginia, felt the cold winter air blowing through the shaft, and smelled the coal dust that can explode on a moment's notice if safe working conditions are not properly maintained.

I have been in a thousand crowded big-city neighborhoods, fast-changing suburbs, farms, towns, and homes. I have come to a new appreciation of the pressures, the concerns, and the hopes of ordinary American workers.

I know that this country is kept going day in and day out by hard-working men and women, not all of whom love their jobs by a long shot but who do them because doing a job well is something to take pride in—in and of itself.

I know that the working people of this country are being asked to give everything for their country—including their sons' lives in a confusing war that no one wants—and feel their government is not giving them much in return.

I know that the majority of the people in this country—whether they are white or black or red or brown—are not bigots or racists.

I know—and you know it, too—that if a man has a job that he thinks has a future and respect, that if his kids are going to school where they can learn, that if his taxes are fair, that if he can take his family out to a park that is not hopelessly polluted, and that if his car doesn't break down two weeks after the dealer delivers it and the dealer then tells him the warranty doesn't cover his particular problem—

If a man has these things, then that man will not really care who works at the next bench or who lives next door.

What the voters of Florida were trying to tell us with that vote for Wallace was that they don't have these things but they want them and intend to get them—if they have to tell off every politician in the country in the process.

Well, that's all right—that's what the political process in this country is all about. In fact, part of our problem is that the only time people think they can express themselves today is in talk shows and elections, because in between the politicians do not want to listen.

I believe that people have a right to expect government to listen. I believe they have a right to have their most basic hopes —a job and a family and a wholesome life—fulfilled to the greatest extent possible by their government.

As Willie Loman's wife said in Arthur Miller's *Death of a Salesman,* "Attention must be paid."

That is what the people in Florida were saying by their vote for Wallace and against bussing—*attention must be paid.*

But here is where I think people have to stop and think—whether voting for George Wallace and stopping the buses is really going to give them all the other things they want: jobs, homes, healthy families, better schools, safe communities—futures they look forward to with pride.

If I thought that voting for George Wallace and stopping the buses—and supporting the President—would deliver these things, then I would vote for them myself.

But I do not believe that is the case.

I do believe that Wallace and the President—and even some of the other Democratic candidates in this race—Humphrey and Jackson—think they are playing a game with the people, with bussing being the thing to take people's minds off the problems which really concern them.

I believe that Wallace and Nixon want people to think so much about bussing that they forget whether they have a job or not; whether the job they have is safe, secure, or bearable; whether their pay raise is higher than their tax increase; whether they can afford the property taxes on their homes and the sales taxes on everything else; whether the streets are dirtier than they used to be; whether their kids are learning to read and write and add—bussing or no bussing.

Bussing is not a race issue.

It is not even a real issue.

I listened very carefully to the President's speech on bussing the other night.

I assume that was the President's response to Mr. Wallace and the vote of the people in Florida.

If it was, the President proved once again that he misses the message the people are trying to get through to all of us.

People are afraid of losing their jobs—if they already haven't. They are afraid of having their neighborhoods go to pieces. They are afraid of the unfair burden of taxes that are higher than they can afford. They are afraid of getting sick because they can't lose a week's wages or be wiped out by hospital bills only the very rich can afford.

The President's solution for all this was one thing—to stop the school bus.

Now you and I know that stopping the bus with political rhetoric is not a solution.

Wallace knows it. Nixon knows it. My friend, Hubert Humphrey, who has climbed on the anti-bussing bandwagon, knows it.

First of all, despite what the President said, the school bus is not going to stop anywhere it is running now—and, most likely, in some places it will begin to run in the future.

I am not saying this because I think the bussing of children is a great idea, though it is true that 42 percent of all schoolchildren in the country get to school by bus, the vast majority of them voluntarily and with nothing to do with integrating the schools racially—just because the bus is pretty much the only way to get there.

Despite that, the President said, the only way he can stop the school buses from running is to upset the whole system of government on which all of us have depended for almost two hundred years. The only way the President can stop the buses from running is by getting the Congress to take away from the courts —from the lowest court to the Supreme Court—the right to interpret and enforce the Constitution of the country. And, despite what the President said, that is just not going to happen.

Even if the Congress passes the legislation the President asked for, the Supreme Court—with the President's own Chief Justice Burger presiding—will find that legislation unconstitutional—as the country's leading constitutional experts have already. After all, this Supreme Court that Nixon is attacking has four of his appointees—and it was his Chief Justice that wrote the bussing decision he now finds unacceptable.

The only way the President can stop the buses from running is to ask the Congress to pass a constitutional amendment, and he did not ask for that—and not just because it would take years to finally pass a constitutional amendment, but because the President knows full well that when you start fooling around with the country's Constitution, you are getting into a very serious and dangerous business.

President Nixon is attempting to use the presidential right to television time to incite public opinion against our judicial system. He is attempting to bring such public pressure on the Congress that it will act unwisely to enact legislation which he knows will be struck down as violating a strict construction of the Constitution. This is but part of a continuing Nixon attack on the courts and on the very basis of our democratic system— the principle of three equal branches sharing the responsibility of government and existing in a delicate balance of power that ensures a fair and final settlement of our disputes.

The threat that this represents goes beyond bussing and the problems of the moment and this presidential election. This has been tried before and defeated because the American people would not tolerate it. Franklin D. Roosevelt tried to pack the U.S. Supreme Court at the height of his political power. He was rebuffed by the American people. Richard Nixon has tried to pack the U.S. Supreme Court. Twice his appointees have been rejected by the U.S. Senate.

Now he is making another—a back-door—attack on the Court which is now dominated by his own appointees. It will be defeated because the American people will not tolerate it.

If the President's political ploy to jam the judiciary to block the school bus were accepted, it would be used tomorrow by this president or some future president to deal with some other issue—perhaps to deprive you or me or our children or grand-children of their God-given rights.

That is why we must unite, shoulder to shoulder, to protect our courts by halting anti-bussing hysteria. It is a threat to our most cherished possession—our heritage of personal conscience and freedom as Americans.

Let me say this clearly for all who will listen: The courts are the fortress walls between the people and those who would work tyranny upon them. Do not undermine them—for the conse-quences will erode the liberty of all Americans.

Let me tell you what I believe is the real reason the President proposed a law that he knows will not work. He did it to make sure that the Congress and the country do nothing else for the rest of the year but endlessly debate bussing. He did it to make sure—as Governor Wallace is trying to make sure—that the working man and woman in America forget about the real problems before the country.

He wants us to forget about the fact that the inflation he proposed to end almost four years ago is still robbing the pay check of every worker in this country. Just go to the supermarket if you don't believe that. He wants us to forget that there are seven or eight million men and women in this country walking the streets for jobs that they cannot find because the President's idea of providing jobs to people is giving big business a $6 billion tax break—while big business gives him $400,000 to run the Republican Convention in San Diego this summer.

He wants us to forget that under his administration, which came into office pledged to a secret plan to end the war, 20,000 young Americans have died in the past three years—most of them sons of working families, many of them with black skins.

These are the things that are the real concerns of the people of the country today—not how long a child has to ride a bus, though the issue of the bus ride has become a temporary symbol of all these grievances rolled into one.

And what about the President's pledge to provide quality education to the ghetto schools by providing $2.5 billion for those schools? First, after the President's brave speech, it turned out that was money already in the budget. Second, we have been spending that kind of money on the schools for years now—without the faintest idea whether it has done any good. Third, last year when Congress passed a multi-billion-dollar education bill to bring money into your schools, President Nixon vetoed that bill as wasteful and inflationary. Now, when he wants to direct attention from this record, he talks of money for quality education.

Mr. Nixon is trying to get the working man to forget the mess he has put the country in.

But the working man is not forgetting anything.

The working citizen is shouting out the laundry list of his problems and he is tired of being taken to the cleaners.

Mr. Nixon tried to tell us the worker was the silent American. Well, he is not silent. He knows his problems and he is saying they better be dealt with—or by God, we'll turn you all out.

That was what the Wallace vote meant—and that is the message Nixon missed.

The people—white, black, red, and brown—are tired of the same old ride. This time—in this election—they want to make sure they are really going someplace that makes sense. They want a real program to turn this country around—to provide jobs and humane working conditions, fair wages and fair taxes, a sound, basic education and a wholesome environment for their children.

The only way that is going to come about is from a real program directed at real change. And, if the Democratic Party wants the vote of working people, it has to offer that kind of program. So I am here tonight to offer that kind of program— the same program I took into the working wards of Manchester, New Hampshire, the same program that won me the support of the voters in those wards.

I am here to offer a program that will really turn this country back to the people where it has always belonged.

One sixty-year-old widow who voted for Governor Wallace in Florida said she did so partly because of disgust with the war continuing to go on.

"Anybody who'd end that war," she said, "I'm with him. But they're all liars."

I wish I'd had a chance to talk to that lady personally— because I think I could have convinced her that I would end that war without delay.

I promise you tonight that if I were president I would end that sad war the day I took the oath of office—and I would make sure that every American prisoner and soldier came home.

I promise you tonight that if I were president not a single American boy would be left to be the last to die in a war everyone else wants to get out of—and not a single father would be put in the position of having to explain to his son why he should be the last to go.

That same widow in Florida, talking about economics, said:

"It's getting so you can't live. You take someone on Social Security, like me. They come in here and put in new sewers and raise taxes, but where do we get the money? The older people are fed up with this government."

And not just the older people. Every young man just out of school who cannot find a first job is fed up. Every working man who has been laid off from his job is fed up. Every wife who has worked part-time to help make ends meet and now cannot find part-time work is fed up—fed up and tired of waiting for the promises of the Nixon Administration to come true.

Working people in this country want no more promises about the economy and jobs. They want performance.

What this country needs is a new Economic Bill of Rights that guarantees every man and woman who is physically able and wants to work, a job at a living wage—and for those who are too old or too sick or too weak to work, an income adequate to meet basic human needs.

Not welfare—but an income.

Old people on Social Security should not have to depend on politicians in Washington to raise their payments when election years roll around. Social Security payments should be tied by law to the cost of living, and whenever those costs go up payments should go up.

A key part of a new Economic Bill of Rights would be comprehensive tax reform that would put more pay in the pockets of the working man and less profit in the ledgers of the big corporations and the vaults of the big banks.

The reason the Nixon Administration has failed so badly to get our economy moving again is that it has failed to understand that it is the income of the average person in this country that is the motor force of economic growth, not the profits of business and the banks.

We could raise $28 billion in new revenues by making sure that every person with income over $50,000 pays a substantial minimum tax, by reducing the special loopholes like the oil depletion allowance and the other gimmicks that let the rich get off without paying any taxes, and by imposing a high tax on inherited fortunes over a half million dollars.

We could raise another $32 billion by cutting out unnecessary wasteful military spending—and still have the strongest defense on the face of the earth. This $32 billion would go into the economy—to increase the number of jobs with a more intelligent use of resources.

The two major economic reforms, tax reform and the cutting of military waste, would raise $60 billion for the national treasury:

Dollars that can be used to reduce high property taxes and make sure every school—in the city as well as in the suburbs—gets the same amount of funding;

Dollars that can be used to end welfare and to provide jobs and dignified income for the needy;

Dollars that can be used to provide a hot school lunch for every schoolchild and one hot meal a day for the old and disabled;

Dollars that can be used to provide the best medical care this country can offer at a reasonable cost;

Dollars that help clean up pollution without forcing industries that keep people working to close down.

America needs new leadership—the kind of leadership that stands up for people.

America does not need the kind of leadership that is ready to make any deal with George Wallace.

Ten years ago, George Wallace was trying to sell a bill of goods to the American people by standing in the schoolhouse door instead of in front of the school bus.

Ten years ago, we had a different kind of national leadership. We had a president who cared about the well-being of all our people.

John Kennedy did not make a deal with Wallace—he stood up to him.

"The heart of the question," President Kennedy said, "is

whether all Americans are to be afforded equal rights and equal opportunities, whether we are going to treat our fellow Americans as we want to be treated. If an American, because his skin is dark . . . cannot lead the full free life which all of us want, then who among us would be content to have the color of his skin changed and stand in his place?"

President Kennedy stood for you—he stood for all of us, from the smallest of us to the biggest, from the politician to the schoolchild, from the steelworker to the teacher, from the machinist to the draftsman.

He offered all of us pride—pride in ourselves, pride in our neighbor, pride in America.

It is time for a return to that kind of leadership. It is time for a return to fair play, self-respect, and pride.

That is the kind of leadership I offer. That is the hope I have for our country.

I ask your help to make the best of America happen again.

The Establishment Center

By April of 1972 I was winning primaries and accumulating the largest delegate totals in non-primary states. My campaign began taking on real importance in the eyes of analysts who had dismissed it before as a hopeless endeavor. So we started hearing a new conventional wisdom —instead of the assertion that I could not possibly be nominated, the claim was that the party had better choose someone who stood as close as possible to President Nixon. This was my response.

Catholic University of America

WASHINGTON, D.C. | APRIL 20, 1972

Prior to the first primary election in New Hampshire, and the most recent one in Wisconsin, the conventional view of men who write and read each other's syndicated columns was that the presidential candidate elected in 1972 would be the one who clings most tightly to the center.

This view—heavily supported by pollsters and analysts of the public mind—held that the American people wanted not a hard-fought battle over the great issues, but a quiet coronation of the status quo.

I have not found this glorification of the establishment center to be the mood of the American people.

Indeed, most Americans see the establishment center as an empty, decaying void that commands neither their confidence nor their love.

It is the establishment center that has led us into the stupidest and cruelest war in all history. That war is a moral and political disaster—a terrible cancer eating away the soul of the nation. Yet those who charted its course brand its opponents as too far out to be electable.

My answer to that is: Nuts! My platform is to stop the bombing of the people of Southeast Asia immediately and then get every American out of Indochina—lock, stock, and barrel—within ninety days.

The establishment center has persisted in seeing the planet as engaged in a gigantic struggle to the death between the free world and the Communist world. The facts are that much of the so-called free world is not free, but a collection of self-seeking military dictators financed by hard-pressed American workers. And most of the Communist nations are far more obsessed with their own internal divisions than they are with Washington, London, Bonn, or Saigon.

Even so, the establishment center has constructed a vast military colossus based on the pay checks of the American worker. That military monster, now capable of blowing up the entire world a hundred times over, is devouring two out of three of our tax dollars. It inflates our economy, picks our pockets, and starves other areas of our national life.

It was not the American worker who designed the Vietnam war or our military machine. It was the establishment wise men, the academicians of the center. As Walter Lippmann once observed: "There is nothing worse than a belligerent professor."

My policy would be to cut the vast waste from our bloated military budget and invest the savings in job-creating enterprises based on a guaranteed job for every man and woman who wants to work.

The Number One economic issue before America today is jobs and more jobs. This nation desperately needs the labor and talent of every man and woman in this land. Nothing is more wasteful than unemployment.

I pledge without qualification that if I become president, I will do whatever is necessary to see that there is a job for every American who wants a job.

It is the establishment center that has erected an unjust tax burden on the backs of American workers while 40 percent of the corporations paid no federal income taxes at all last year. I say that is an outrage.

I propose to close $28 billion in tax loopholes for the rich and the powerful and use the savings to reduce property taxes, strengthen our schools, and rebuild our cities.

It is the establishment center that tells us we can afford an ABM, but we cannot afford good health care for the American people.

I say that is intolerable.

It is the establishment center that says we can afford a $250 million guaranteed loan to Lockheed, but we cannot afford a decent retirement income for our senior citizens.

And I say that is intolerable.

It is the establishment center that says it is okay to tell the American people one thing in public while plotting a different course in secret.

I say it is time to close the credibility gap and begin telling the American people the truth.

The people of this country are not left or right or centrist. Rather, they seek a way out of the wilderness.

And if we who seek their trust, trust them enough to speak the plain truth, the people will find their own way.

Down the long and often troubled history of this great republic, the people have never been found lacking in imagination, resourcefulness, courage, and generosity. Given a leadership responsive to the best in their nature and equal to the demands of their essential goodness, they will work their way through to a just, compassionate, and well-ordered society. To say this, for me, is to state a simple faith in the unique quality of the American people.

What is needed is a revitalization of the American center based on the enduring ideals of the republic. The present center has drifted so far from our founding ideals that it bears little resemblance to the dependable values of the Declaration of Independence and the Constitution. I want America to come home from the alien world of power politics, militarism, deception, racism, and special privilege to the blunt truth that "all men are created equal, that they are endowed by their creator with certain inalienable rights, that among these are life, liberty, and the pursuit of happiness."

I want the new coalition at the center to burn with such a reverence for life that we will end senseless wars, offer jobs to the jobless, food for the hungry, housing for the homeless, and health care for the sick.

I want a new coalition at the center with such a passion for liberty that all people—black, brown, red, and white—male and female—young and old—will know the reality of liberation.

I want the pursuit of happiness to reach the despairing Vietnam veteran, the lonely old person, the drug addict, the prison inmate, the overburdened taxpayer, the forgotten worker, the little farmer and merchant; in short, I want all of us to have the assurance that we live in a nation where we care deeply about each other. That was the spirit of the Continental Congress, that was the spirit that opened the American frontier, that is the way home for America to a rallying center to which all Americans can repair.

It is not left or right to demand an end to deception in government. It is not left or right to demand a job opportunity for every American. It is not left or right to demand that government become more responsive to the frustrations of ordinary citizens. It is not left or right to demand a tax structure that requires the rich and the powerful to pay their fair share. It is not left or right to demand that all Americans be treated with equal dignity without regard to race, creed, or sex.

It is not left or right to demand an end to the pollution of our planet. It is not left or right to demand that we convert military waste to those ends that glorify life. It is not left or right to demand an end to a pointless and costly war.

Twenty-five hundred years ago, the biblical sage wrote:

"I have set before you two choices—life or death, blessing or cursing. Therefore, choose life, that thou and thy seed may live."

I want this nation we all love to turn away from cursing and hatred and war to the blessings of hope and brotherhood and love.

Let us choose life, that we and our children may live. Then our children will love America not simply because it is theirs but because of the great and good land all of us together have made it.

A Vision of America

It is easy to discuss specific issues in a campaign. It is harder to describe a vision of the country's future without descending into clichés or ascending into abstractions. I made an attempt to provide this harder description at the Truman Day Dinner in St. Louis. The speech was the product of long thought and concentrated work. It distilled many of my most deeply held beliefs about America. The occasion on which it was delivered was also significant because it was the first public meeting between Senator Eagleton and me since Sargent Shriver had replaced him on the ticket.

Truman Day Award Dinner
ST. LOUIS, MISSOURI | OCTOBER 7, 1972

There are several reasons why I especially want to win the 1972 election in Missouri. First of all, this is Harry Truman's state and I would like to demonstrate, as he did, that the people of this country can still upset the polls and the pundits.

Secondly, I have had a special relationship with the Symington family for many years. Stuart Symington, one of the most respected men in the Senate, has helped me win hard-fought campaigns in South Dakota. His son, Congressman Jim Symington, was my deputy in Food for Peace during those bright early months of the administration of John F. Kennedy.

Then I especially want to win in Missouri because of Tom Eagleton. No matter what others may think, there will always be a special bond between the Eagletons and the McGoverns that is only possible when two families go through a difficult and heartrending experience together. I do not say that we handled this matter every step of the way as wisely as possible. But if there were mistakes, they were honest mistakes of the heart.

To those who are troubled that a presidential candidate could back his chosen running mate 1,000 percent and then ask him to step down a week later, I can only say that in politics as in life, compassion must sometimes yield to more reflective and painful judgment.

To those who object to a presidential candidate publicly changing his mind, I say that a leader who would rather save face than respond to new insight is no leader at all; he is a disaster—as witness our sad experience in Vietnam.

I took the hard course that I believe was in the national interest—a course that was only possible with Tom's respect and cooperation.

We wanted this campaign to center—not on the issue of one man's medical history—but on the great issues of war and peace, the American economy, the quality of our society, and the condition of our constitutional government.

With so many significant issues confronting our nation, any American who makes his judgment in 1972 on the basis of an incident that Tom Eagleton and I have now put behind us, is betraying his obligations to responsible citizenship.

Tom Eagleton is on the way to enhanced national stature. And we can put our nation on the way to enhanced national stature if we take the government out of the hands of Richard Nixon and his special-interest friends and restore it to the people of America.

The stakes in 1972 reach beyond the problems of the movement to overriding questions about the future of America.

What kind of country are we?

What kind of country do we want to be?

What kind of life should we seek together?

My answer is the same as James Russell Lowell's when he was asked a century ago: "How long do you think the American Republic will last?"

He replied: "So long as the ideas of the Founding Fathers continue to be dominant."

Our nation was born in a noble vision of human existence. The pilgrims named their land New England because they hoped to found a new order. Our forebears inscribed the Great Seal of the United States with the words: "A New Order for the Ages." And on that seal, a pyramid, which stands for material wealth, supports a symbol which stands for spiritual strength.

So the new order of America was to be based on an abundance that freed men to find meaning in their lives as well as a livelihood for their families. In the American vision, life was supposed to be more than an exhausting effort to exist, more than material comfort and success.

Our forbears affirmed that people have a right to purpose and fulfillment—a right to glory in their dreams.

And the faith of our forefathers was cherished by millions who followed after them. From a hundred different lands and every continent, immigrants came to America—not because they believed the streets were paved with gold, and not merely for jobs and economic opportunity—but because here they hoped to find a new birth of freedom for themselves and their children, a new liberation of the spirit.

Now, after centuries of struggle, we have become the strongest and the richest society in human history. The ancient dream is within our grasp—the dream that here, at long last, will be one place on this planet where all those who are willing to work for it can find freedom from want and war.

Yet, in the midst of these wonders, even in sight of this boundless material abundance, our spirit languishes.

In suburbs as well as slums, our children turn to drugs as they turn away from us. More and more families break up, neighborhoods decline, traditions and values are lost. Workers find themselves feeling irritable and frustrated because the system created to serve them only exhausts them, bores them, uses them up, and exploits them. Our miraculous technology mocks us as it pollutes our land, our air, and water. And the divisions among us grow deeper instead of fewer—divisions of age and race and class.

It is said that young people these days are alienated. But so are many embittered elderly and angry middle-aged, and the cynical and self-indulgent of every age. It is said that blacks feel shut out of the system. But so do whites and Spanish-speaking peoples and citizens of every race, religion, and nationality. It is said that the poor feel scorned, ignored and put upon. But so do union members and housewives and intellectuals and returning veterans and all the restless dissatisfied people of this land.

We are doubtful and even suspicious of each other. We wonder why nothing seems to work right any more. We wonder whether America has gained the world, only to lose its soul.

But I believe we can make America hope once again.

We cannot do it with words of easy assurance. We cannot recover our greatness and happiness merely by saying that we have no difficulties.

War cannot be ended by calling it peace. Recession cannot be solved by calling it prosperity. America cannot be perfected by those who say it is already perfect.

Do you really believe, as our opponents tell you, that the American nation is now what it was and could be and should be?

Do you really believe, as our opponents tell you, that the American spirit today is refreshed and hopeful and satisfied?

Do you really believe, as our opponents tell you, that America can go on as it has for four more years?

They would do well to remember the words of the ancient orator: "Our trouble is with those who would please us instead of serving us."

The way for the next president to serve us is by restoring America to its founding principles.

The first and most fundamental principle is that government and the people must be united by a bond of mutual confidence. Nothing any president says will make any difference if the people distrust him. None of his individual programs or the most eloquent speeches matter half so much as the character of his leadership.

The next president cannot summon America to a higher standard unless he sets a higher standard himself. He cannot persuade Americans to care about their fellow human beings unless he cares. It will take time to convince the people that this has been done. For too long, we have been given rhetoric without reality and promises that were made to be broken. All politicians and presidents are suspect in 1972.

On a visit to a hospital in Vietnam last year, a terribly disillusioned and badly wounded young Marine told me: "I will never again trust the government."

Only a president who keeps faith with the people can in time revive their confidence in government.

He can insist on an administration that is not for sale to any special interest. He can disclose the names of all his campaign contributors. He can share the great decisions of war and peace and taxation with the Congress and the people. He can put a halt to the deceit and manipulation involved in officials advocating one course in public while plotting a different course in secret.

Finally, the next president can restore trust in government only if he himself trusts the people to face the facts and see the truth. A commitment to openness has a price. No president and no candidate is immune from error; an open campaign and an open administration will inevitably expose every mistake to public view. But better the obvious mistakes of honest leadership than the cold and apparent efficiency of a leadership which blinds us to its blunders until disaster is upon us.

It has been recently said that people will accept lies, corruption, and even burglary in high places because they expect nothing better. That is tragic, if it is true. But if the next president demands integrity in every part of government, then so will citizens demand and expect a government that corrects evil instead of committing it.

Yet, this is only the first step. The critical question is what the next president does with the trust he earns.

The president's job is to act, not merely react; to lead, not merely follow public opinion; to help bring the country forward, not merely be dragged along with it. Above all, he must care— as Abraham Lincoln cared about the widows of war, and Franklin Roosevelt cared about the hungry and poor, as John Kennedy cared about the jobless, and Harry Truman cared about the little people of America and the world.

That is the kind of president that I want to be. That is the kind of president that, God willing, I will be.

There will be no more White House indifference to scandal in high office. As president of the United States, I shall appoint to my cabinet and administration men and women of the highest honor, ability, and character, regardless of party; and I shall promptly remove anyone guilty of misfeasance or malfeasance, regardless of politics.

There will be no more White House indifference to generals conducting and expanding and prolonging a war on their own. Our system calls for civilian control over the military; and as your president and commander-in-chief, I will control the military.

There will be no more White House indifference to the poor and oppressed among us; to those who protest, or those who suffer in silence; to the women who are seeking a more fulfilling role in American society; to the young who are in a hurry for change and to the black or brown or red who can wait no longer for change. No single group's voice in this diverse country must always be heeded; but every voice must always be heard. As president of all Americans, I will hear those voices of dissent and discontent and offer them hope for a better world.

This is what I offer—not four more years of doubt and drift and indifference, but a determination to call America home to the old values of brotherhood and personal dignity, neighborhood and nationhood.

Almost every country in the world is a country because its people share a common culture. They speak the same language, read the same poetry, and dance to the same music. Their roots are in one land.

America is different. America is a land of diversity discovered by an Italian commissioned by the queen of Spain. Our independence was won by men named Kosciusko, Von Steuben, and Lafayette, as well as Jefferson, Adams, and Paine. Our land has been tilled, our factories have been worked, and our cities have been served by the Poles, the Germans, the Scandinavians, the Greeks, the East Europeans, and all the others. Chinese Americans built the transcontinental railroad from the West, and at Promontory Point in Utah they met Irish-Americans who were building it from the East. Our culture has been diversified and enriched by the American Indians, the black Americans, and the Spanish-surnamed Americans. Every language that is heard in the world today has been heard within our borders. Every religious creed finds its free expression here.

We are a country founded not on a common culture, but on common ideals. There is perhaps no other place on this planet that is a country solely because of a set of ideas. And if we lose that, we will be just a collection of people going our different ways.

In short, if I win this election, I would like to be remembered most of all for restoring the presidency to a moral leadership worthy of a great people. Moral leadership does not tell people something they do not know; it asks them to look into their own souls for the truth that is already there.

No president can give an individual the fulfillment he must find for himself. But a president can lift the vision of the nation; he can honor its enduring values of family, moral integrity, and the essential worth of every human being.

He can fight to feed the hungry, to employ the jobless, to cure the addicted, to house the homeless, to ease the monotony and drudgery of the factory, to strengthen independent business and family agriculture against the concentration of corporate power —so that people will be able to truly seek what is deepest in their hearts.

He can—he must—and as president, I will—summon America back to a sense of shared purpose and great enterprise.

Just as thirty years ago Rosie the Riveter was convinced that she was helping to win World War Two—and she was right— all of us, whether we are professors or policemen, bricklayers or business executives, whatever we are, must be helped by our leaders to see how our efforts can help make America hope once again.

We need to believe that our work as individuals has worth and dignity—that it is not just aimless, daily drudgery, but an indispensable contribution to a better land and life for ourselves and our children.

You will not always agree with a president who exercises tough moral leadership. The voters of South Dakota did not agree with me when I first spoke out against the Vietnam war nine years ago.

Yet I believe that Americans want a president who will tell them the hard truths as well as the easy ones—who will appeal not just to our selfish interests, but to what Lincoln called "the better angels of our nature."

Deep down, we all understand that democracy is corrupted by a political leadership that puts greedy special interests above the well-being of the people.

Deep down, we know our constitutional system is weakened by a leadership that degrades the Supreme Court, ignores the warmaking power of Congress, or destroys our privacy with the wiretap and the official eavesdropper.

Deep down, we all understand that racial injustice is wrong— and that we must right the injustice of ignoring it if we want America to truly be America again.

Deep down, we do not want to be a vindictive and mean-spirited people—and after peace brings all our sons home from Indochina, our generosity of spirit must not only care more generously for those who have borne the battle, but also reach out to repatriate others among our sons who in conscience could not fight this war.

A month from now, you will choose the next president of the United States. I think I know how you will decide.

I am behind in the polls, as I was in the spring. I am short of money, as I was in the spring. But I believe we will win in the fall, as we did in the spring.

I believe this because I have been out in the country, campaigning among the people. I have traveled this land for twenty months, in quest of the presidency and in search of a vision for America.

I have looked into the eyes of people from Maine to California. I have listened to them and tried to sense what is in their hearts.

And this is what I have learned. The people are not left, or right, or center. Rather, they seek a way out of the wilderness.

They want those who seek their trust to trust them, so they can find their own way.

They want an open government and open politics.

They want to cherish this country, to take pride in what it does, to honor what it represents.

They want a leadership that asks the best of us, so we can glow with a new love for America—and America can lift a new light to all the world.

That is what I have seen among you.

That is why I am confident that we will win not only a victory in November—but a rebirth for our nation in the years ahead.

Then our children and their children after them will love America not merely because they were born here—but because of the great and good and proud land that you and I together have made it.

Thank you, and God bless you.

Sources of Our Strength

During the campaign I explicitly addressed the theme of ethics and public affairs in a broader context. Of course, that theme was often sounded in other speeches—too often, in the view of some observers. But I am convinced now, as I was last year, that our problem is not too much morality in politics, but too much politics without morality.

Wheaton College

WHEATON, ILLINOIS | OCTOBER 11, 1972

Recently, someone sent me a radio sermon delivered by the Reverend Joel Nederhood of *The Back to God Hour* broadcast from Chicago. The sermon was about the faith of our presidents. Dr. Nederhood contended that Americans have adopted the dangerous custom of separating religion from their evaluation of national leaders.

He said:

"To suggest that one's faith might influence a person in his discharge of public office, apparently, is akin to suggesting that the man is guilty of dishonorable conflict of interest. Thus, while candidates for public office often claim some kind of membership in a religious body, they ordinarily disavow any connection between their faith and their views of public policy."

I believe this is wrong for a nation whose founders were so deeply motivated by religious conviction.

We all stand for the constitutional principle of separation of church and state. But we should all stand against the distortion of this principle into the practice of separating faith from politics, and morality from government.

So I have accepted your invitation to come here to Wheaton College because I want to talk about the moral dimenisons of our life as a nation.

I have no intention of giving you a "political" speech. I suspect, in fact, that you are far less interested in my "politics," per se, than in how my religious convictions have shaped my view of America's difficulties and our destiny.

My father attended Houghton College in New York and was ordained as a minister in the Wesleyan Methodist Church, an evangelical, fundamentalist faith. In our family, there was no drinking, smoking, dancing, or card playing. So you can see why I feel so much at home here at Wheaton.

In all candor, I regard that kind of strict legalism as somewhat beside the point today and as not a necessary or totally positive part of a Christian upbringing.

But that was not the whole picture.

In our home, the family gathered every morning to read Scripture. In fact, I remember how my father taught me to read aloud from the Bible before I was old enough to go to school. We spent Sunday at Sunday School, at church, listening to our father's sermons, followed by a children's worship service, and then a prayer meeting. It is from these experiences that I have some of the most vivid and vital memories of my past. Daily teaching from the Scripture, and a constant immersion in faith, made an indelible impression.

I went through a period of mild rebellion against some of the rigidity of my early years. But then, after my service in World War Two as a bomber pilot, a pattern started to unfold in my life. I felt called into the work of serving others. At first I thought that my vocation was in the ministry, and I enrolled in seminary. During that year, I served as a student pastor for a church in Diamond Lake, Illinois, north of Chicago. It was a year that left me with fresh insight about the demands of religious leadership, and a time when I grew in many ways. I thought about my vocation, for I knew, as my mother told me, that a man should not go into the ministry unless he was certain God was calling him there.

And after a period of deep reflection, I decided that I should become a teacher. Yet, even in my teaching at Dakota Wesleyan University, I still felt that there was something else for me to do —and that is what finally led me into politics.

The Bible teaches that government is to serve man, not that men are the servants of government.

When the New Testament speaks of "honoring those in authority," for instance, it points out that power is ordained by God for the purpose of doing good for the people.

In this light, I have come to understand the responsibility of of political office, and the opportunities for service which it holds.

But we must also recognize a central fact: All that we seek in our society will not come solely from government.

The greatest challenges of our age defy purely political answers.

I remember the Civil Rights March of 1963, which was followed by the historic passage of the Civil Rights Act a year later. Many Americans hoped that this single act would set us on a rapid course toward the extinction of racial prejudice. But the real crisis was still ahead of us—and it is still unresolved. In the last decade, we have learned that discrimination is rooted in attitudes, and frustrations, and fears that cannot be dispelled by law, but in our hearts. There is much that can and must be done by government; but much more must be done by each of us in our own lives.

The war in Indochina could be ended at any moment by the

president of the United States. As I pointed out last night, it can be ended by the simple choice of different policies.

But what about the attitudes that brought us to this war?

What about the insensitivity of those who have given us weekly body counts—who have told us in effect that one death is a tragedy, and thousands are a statistic?

What about the tears shed over the death of Americans, while too many seem indifferent to death among the Vietnamese?

What about the weapons of mass destruction which deny our belief in the sanctity of human life?

We can change our course, and make peace, as I am committed to do. But we must also change those things in our national character which turned us astray, away from the truth that the people of Vietnam are, like us, children of God.

As president, I could not resolve all the problems of this land. No president and no political leader can.

For our deepest problems are within us—not as an entire people, but as individual persons.

So Christians have a responsibility to speak to the questions of the spirit which ultimately determine the state of the material world. Most Americans yearn for meaning and value in life. This is a preeminent task for those who are in the church—but it cannot be separated from what happens outside the church.

Some Christians believe that we are condemned to live with man's inhumanity to man—with poverty, war, and injustice—and that we cannot end these evils because they are inevitable.

But I have not found that view in the Bible.

Changed men can change society, and the words of Scripture clearly assign to us the ministry and the mission of change.

While we know that the Kingdom of God will not come from a political party's platform, we also know if someone is hungry we should give him food; if he is thirsty, we should give him drink; if he is a stranger we should take him in; if he is naked we should clothe him; if he is sick we should care for him; and if he is in prison we should visit him. "For inasmuch as you have done it unto the least of these my brethren, you have done it unto me."

That is what Scripture says. None of us can be content until all of us are made whole.

This is also the lesson in the lives of the great evangelists.

Jonathan Edwards is remembered for his role in the Great Awakening that swept colonial America. But few realize that he was so dedicated to the struggle against suffering and disease that he offered himself to test a smallpox vaccine. And in this act of charity and love and sacrifice, he died.

John Wesley set up clinics to bring medical care to the deprived citizens of London.

In the 1800's, one of the great evangelists, William Wilberforce, was a leader in the abolitionist movement, fighting for human freedom.

And we could go on, to Charles Finney and to others.

But even more to the point are the forward movements in society which were at least partly impelled by authentic "awakenings" and "revivals."

The most notable advances of the eighteenth and nineteenth centuries—the fight for decent labor conditions and against slavery, and the efforts for prison reform—seemed to flow from the evangelical tides in society which preceded and accompanied them. Breakthroughs occurred in overcoming inhumanity and injustice because individuals had become infused with a compassion for others—and, even more than that, because the conscience of the nation had been touched and enlivened.

Today, the conscience of our nation must be touched anew.

Arnold Toynbee has written that all the great civilizations of history have fallen not to conquering armies from without, but to a deterioration of spirit from within.

Toynbee asserts that America "now stands for what Rome stood for." I believe that is so in many ways. America, too, is a country of enormous wealth. Our people, like the ancient Romans, seem to live more and more for materialistic satisfaction. Standards of morality and precious values are in disarray as they were then. And like the Roman Empire that ruled the world, our power is engaged far from our homeland, fighting for military influence in impoverished lands.

Toynbee concludes: "Affluence is estranging America from her own ideals. It is pushing her into the position of being the leader of the very opposite of what America's World Revolution stands for."

We must have a fundamental stirring of our moral and spiritual values if we are to reclaim our true destiny. That kind of awakening can free us from a relentless devotion to material affluence, with too much for some citizens and too little for others. It can free us from a blind trust in armed might. It can free us from a dogmatic faith in salvation through technology.

Such an awakening can also stir our compassion for others, restore the commitment of lives and give us happiness.

We must look into our souls to find the way out of the crisis of our society. As was so often true for the people of God in Biblical days, we must heed the words of the prophets.

The New Testament tells us: "Be not conformed to the world, but be you transformed by the renewing of your minds."

Some Christians have misused this passage as a pretext for isolation from the world.

The political process tends to reflect and channel spiritual trends. There are encouraging signs in our land that we are undergoing a new "awakening." The sophisticated "God Is Dead" talk now seems as irrelevant as a passing fad—which is what it was. Instead, the Jesus Movement and other manifestations of spiritual hunger summon millions back to belief.

Within the institutional church and outside of any traditional religious framework, we witness a spiritual quest of increasing intensity. Even those who are uncertain about where this search should end are certain of the need to seek the deeper truth. Others wander through an inner wilderness to find their faith.

Because spiritual currents are moving across our land, I am

hopeful for our future. I believe that these currents must reach into our public life as well as our own souls.

The president can exercise a profound influence to this end. I believe that it is his most serious responsibility.

The president can be the great moral leader of the nation. He can ask us to face issues, not merely from a political standpoint, but in our conscience and our souls.

By his words and deeds, the president must witness to the values that should endure among our people.

The president must set an uncompromised standard of truth and integrity, for if these principles are corrupted at the highest levels of government, corruption will spread to other levels of society.

Finally, the president must have within his heart a vision of what America should be, of the true calling of this country. And that vision must be at the very center of all he does. He must see a new day for our people, and labor to bring us there.

Power cannot be his only purpose. There is no virtue in simply "being president." A candidate should seek the presidency to serve the nation, and call it to a higher standard.

This is the meaning of true leadership. It is not expressed in power, fame, and honor, but in the washing of dusty feet.

We know that "he who saves his life shall lose it."

And he who seeks the presidency should not be willing to pay any price. He must do so in allegiance to his principles and his faith. "For what shall it profit a man if he should gain the whole world, but lose his own soul?"

America was founded as part of a spiritual pilgrimage. It was born in a noble vision of human existence. The first settlers named their land New England because they hoped to found a new order. Our forebears inscribed the Great Seal of the United States with the words "A New Order for the Ages." And on that seal, a pyramid, which stands for material wealth.

So the new order of America was to be based on an abundance that freed men to find meaning in their lives as well as a livelihood for their families. In the American vision, life was supposed to be more than an exhausting effort to exist, more than material comfort and success.

Our forebears stood against the eternal night and affirmed that there is a purpose to life—that people can find fulfillment and glory in their dreams. And the wish of our forebears was to see the way of God prevail.

We have strayed from their pilgrimage, like lost sheep.

But I believe we can begin this ancient journey anew.

In 1630, John Winthrop preached a sermon on the deck of the *Arabella* to the first Puritans. He said:

"We shall be as a city upon a hill, the eyes of all people upon us; so that if we shall deal falsely with our God in this work we have undertaken and so cause him to withdraw His present help from us; we shall be made a story and a by-word through the world."

I believe we can still deal truly, and righteously, with the great gifts that have been ours since the time the Puritans reached these shores. But this will come only after a struggle that touches all our hearts, and is resolved there.

The prophet gives us God's promise:

"If my people which are called by my name, shall humble themselves, and pray, and seek my face, and turn from their wicked ways, then will I hear from heaven, and will forgive their sins, and will heal their land."

So what then do we do? What is your responsibility, and what is mine? Micah asked and answered the same question in a verse I have remembered since my childhood, and turned back to ever since:

"What doth the Lord require of thee, but to do justly, and to love mercy and to talk kindly with thy God."

The Renewal of the Presidency

This speech was developed and discussed for a long time —probably too long, for what it said needed to be heard earlier in the campaign. I am afraid that postponing it until November 5 meant that it probably was not heard at all. But I am more certain than ever that the kind of renewed presidency I outlined—less regal and more responsive, open and not omnipotent—is essential to the nation.

ST. LOUIS, MISSOURI | NOVEMBER 5, 1972

In forty-eight hours, the people will choose the next president.

They will decide between war in Asia and peace for America, between jobs for our workers and favors for the special interests, between four more years of code words and a real attack on crime, between a candidate who hides in the White House and a candidate who has been among the people.

Tuesday will be a day of reckoning and judgment.

And each citizen will decide in his own way.

Those who labor for a living may care more about the economy than any other issue. The young are still stirred most by the unending outrage of Vietnam. A housewife may look at the ballot and think of last week's grocery bill. The old may see their loneliness aggravated by poverty.

For every group, there is an issue and a problem they seek to resolve by their vote.

This is as it should be. People should test their leadership by its immediate impact on their individual lives.

Yet this cannot be the only test. For we are not electing a set of programs, but a president of the United States. And a candidate should be tested above all else by his view of presidential leadership and his vision for the nation.

This is an issue that encompasses and transcends all others. It includes the crises still unseen but certain to come in the next four years, as well as the questions that have been so intensely debated in recent months.

Therefore, I would like to talk with you today, in the closing hours of this campaign, not just about the policies I propose, but about the kind of president I intend to be.

First, I intend to be a people's president.

I intend to fight for rank-and-file Americans against powerful predators of special privilege, both in government and in the private economy.

Government has become so vast and impersonal that its interests diverge more and more from the interests of ordinary citizens. What may save an administration's face or feed its sense of honor, or give it more authority does not necessarily serve or fulfill or enrich the people.

Unfortunately, my opponent—who likes to call himself a conservative—has lost sight of this conservative truth.

He believes in trickle-down power as much as trickle-down economics. And both of those are wrong.

The right course is for a president to champion all the American people rather than the privileged few, no matter how entrenched they are or how far their influence reaches. It is time for a president who will bring the government back to the people.

Second, I intend to conduct an open presidency.

We must end the manipulation and concealment which characterize my opponent's misuse of the White House.

In a democratic nation, no one likes to say that his inspiration came from secret arrangements behind closed doors. But in a sense, that is how my candidacy began twenty-two months ago. I am here today as the Democratic nominee in large part because during four administrations of both parties, a terrible war has been charted behind closed doors.

I want those doors opened, and I want that war closed. And I make this pledge above all others: That war will be closed, and those doors will be opened.

And unlike Mr. Nixon, I will hold regular and frequent press conferences as president.

I will abolish the office of White House director of communications, which my opponent created to censor news and views —not only from inside the White House, but from anywhere in the executive branch.

That office is the first permanent propaganda ministry in the history of this country. It is a dangerous precedent. I plan to make it the fading memory of a mistaken past.

I will also end the insidious practice of hiding facts—not to protect national security, but to preserve the prestige of those who have failed the nation. The truth belongs to the people, and it is stolen property only when it is concealed from them.

But I am not satisfied that any administration, whatever its intentions, can fully police itself to prevent official lies and distortions.

Therefore, I will work closely with editors, news directors, and reporters to develop new and effective checks on government misinformation.

Third, I intend to conduct a presidency of personal responsibility.

As a first step, I will drastically reduce the sprawling, largely unsupervised White House staff. It has become a dangerous and arrogant bureaucracy. It has doubled since Mr. Nixon took office.

Without this increase in size in the last four years, there would not have been idle hands around for the Watergate bugging and burglary, and the unprecedented political espionage conceived and conducted by the Nixon White House.

Nor, as chief executive, will I permit a presidential aide to become involved with a government agency on behalf of ITT or any other corporation.

There will be no more White House indifference to scandal in high places. I will appoint officials of honor, ability, and character, regardless of party. And I will remove any official guilty of misfeasance or malfeasance, regardless of politics.

It has been said recently that people will accept corruption and even criminal activity in the political process because they expect nothing better. That is tragic, if it is true. But if the next president demands integrity in every part of government, then so will citizens demand and expect a government that corrects evils instead of committing them.

But cutting the White House staff and setting a standard of honesty in public service are just the first steps toward a presidency of personal responsibility. The president must not only exert personal supervision over his most important subordinates, he must also have personal contact with rank-and-file Americans.

I find my opponent's conduct of the presidency cold and aloof. He deals too much with the power brokers and too little with the people.

As president, I will go to the country several times a year for town meetings in school auditoriums, factories, and neighborhoods. I will listen as well as speak—and hopefully, I will learn what the people are thinking and feeling.

There will be no more White House indifference to the poor and oppressed among us; to the women who are seeking a more fulfilling role in society; to the young who are in a hurry for change and to the black or brown or red who can wait no longer for change. And the White House will not be deaf to the plight of blue-collar workers who find that the system created to serve them exhausts them, bores them, uses them up, and exploits them. No citizen of this country should have to suffer in silence; no single voice can always be heeded. But every voice must be heard. As president, I will hear the voices of dissent and discontent, and the needs a president will never know if he hides in the White House.

The president is a person, and the presidency is a personal as well as a political institution. The president is personally responsible for those he chooses to serve with him, and for the choice of the voices and views that influence him.

It is wrong for a president to listen just to oil barons and billionaires and the executives of big business. My opponent prefers to go to John Connally's ranch to talk with those who can pay $1,000 for dinner. I will go to the workers on the assembly line at General Motors and the machinists who work at McDonnell-Douglas.

Fourth, I intend to conduct a constitutional presidency.

I will share the deliberations of my administration with both the Congress and the country.

Neither sound decision-making nor the strength of our society is well served when a president relies almost entirely on a handful of generals, bureaucrats, and staff aides to resolve great questions about our economy, our environment, and even our fate.

That is wrong. Yet that is the pattern of my opponent's presidency.

The Constitution says that the executive and legislative branches shall be equal partners. But we are now deep into a long-developing constitutional crisis which threatens us with a government of executive supremacy—or what in old-fashioned terms was called one-man rule. We have seen our democracy diminished by a war that was undeclared, and an invasion of Cambodia that was ordered without the consent of the Congress —indeed, without even consulting the leadership of the Senate and the House.

At the same time, we have seen our courts demeaned, not

so much by the contempt of a few defendants, but by the misconduct of those who are sworn to defend the Constitution—which makes the judiciary the third equal branch of government. Instead, this administration has made the Supreme Court a plaything of partisanship. They have tried to reshape the meaning of the Constitution to fit a strategy of politics. My opponent even attempted to appoint to the Supreme Court a man whose most famous public remark was a racial slur.

Now we must return to the constitutional system of shared authority and lively checks and balances. We must restore respect for the place and power of the courts and the Congress.

We must make the Cabinet the reality of executive government, instead of its shadow.

Executive privilege should never be invoked to escape executive responsibility. I believe that the officials who are responsible for policy should be responsive to the representatives of the people, who have a right to review that policy.

And I believe in a presidency of shared authority in an even more fundamental sense. The president of the United States should take the country into his confidence at an early stage on domestic issues and, to the maximum practical extent, on international initiatives as well.

My opponent breaks into prime television time only to tell the nation what has already been decided.

As president, I will speak regularly to the country about major questions, so citizens as well as the government can think seriously and react before decisions are made.

Instead of ruling like a Roman emperor, I offer a candid presidency, sensitive to our constitutional system and to the concerns of our people.

It is the only real and abiding way to make democracy work.

Fifth, I intend to be a president who puts his primary emphasis on our problems here at home, not on power politics abroad.

I believe the president has fateful responsibilities in our own country and around the world. But we need a better balance between the blind isolationism of the 1930's and the costly over-commitments and indiscriminate interventionism of the 1960's.

We must end the tragic and immoral war in Southeast Asia. Then we must pull our own country together and put our own house in order.

We cannot do so with a president who proudly proclaims that he spends 80 percent of his time on foreign affairs. We need a president who cares more about a father who is out of work in St. Louis than about a corrupt dictator in Saigon who should have been out of power years ago.

The oldest con game in history is for a head of state to avoid the difficulties of his own land by diverting public attention to grand alliances and exaggerated dangers in other lands.

This has worsened during the last four years. I will not let it continue for four more years.

As president, I will give America a defense second to none. I will keep this country strong in military power, but I will not tolerate waste in the Pentagon any more than I will in any other branch of the government. I want to make America strong not only militarily, but in the quality of life. I want the jobless employed, the homeless housed, the hungry fed, and the sick treated.

It will not be easy. But I will fight as Franklin Roosevelt fought, and Harry Truman and Lyndon Johnson and John Kennedy. And we will prevail. We will enact national health insurance. We will reform taxes. We will provide a job for every man and woman in this country who is able to work. We will declare all-out war on crime and drugs. We will halt the contamination of our environment. We will end the neglect of the old and the handicapped. With the support of the people and the commitment of the presidency, we will bring the American deed closer to the American creed.

Finally, I intend to be an innovative and forward-looking president.

For a generation and more, the government has sought to meet our needs by multiplying its bureaucracy.

Washington has taken too much in taxes from Main Street, and Main Street has received too little in return.

It is not necessary to centralize power in order to solve our problems. At other times in our history, government has given people the tools, and they have finished the task.

We must be as innovative as our forebears were when they passed the Homestead Act and the Land Grant College Act under Abraham Lincoln—or the Rural Electrification Act and the TVA under President Roosevelt—or the Peace Corps under John Kennedy.

The first of these, for instance, used public resources, not to subsidize huge government contractors like Lockheed, but to open the opportunity on the frontier for ordinary citizens to earn their own way.

The Land Grant College Act created institutions to educate the sons and daughters of the people that were closer to people than to the bureaucracies in Washington.

And rural electric cooperatives owned and operated by farmers may teach us important lessons about rebuilding our neglected urban neighborhoods.

As president, I will seek innovations to meet the challenges of the 1970's—whether to cut property taxes, or to improve schools, or to achieve full employment through new and novel arrangements with the private sector.

In short, we must make fresh starts on how government works—because government is not working today.

My opponent uncritically clings to bloated bureaucracies, both civilian and military. And at the same time, he opposes vital advances because he says they would further enlarge the bureaucracy.

I believe we must cut out the deadwood of government, decentralize our system, and in this way face up to the problems of the present and the possibilities of the future.

So it is the presidency which must be renewed. And that is what I propose to do in the next four years.

A president must ask the country to do what is right, not

what is easy; to be concerned, not comfortable; to be compassionate, not complacent. Moral leadership does not tell people something they do not know; it asks them to look into their own hearts for the truth that is already there.

For twenty-two months, I have traveled this land in quest of the presidency and in search of a vision for America.

I have looked into the eyes of people from Maine to California. I have listened to them and tried to sense what is in their hearts.

And this is what I have learned.

The people want an open presidency, an open government, and an open politics.

They want to cherish this country, to take pride in what it does, to honor what it represents.

They want a president who demands the best of us, so we can glow with a new love for America—and America can lift a new light before the world.

That is what I have seen among you.

That is why I am confident that we will win—not only a victory in November, but a renewal of the presidency and a rebirth for our nation in the years ahead.

Then our children and their children after them will love America—not merely because they were born here, but because of the great and good land that you and I together have made it.

Thank you, and God bless you.

Pressing the Case

September 12 marked Senator Kennedy's first appearance with me on the campaign trail. It was in Minneapolis, and the auditorium was packed to the rafters. My remarks that night became the basis for many of the "stump speeches" I delivered in the weeks ahead.

MINNEAPOLIS, MINNESOTA | SEPTEMBER 11, 1972

Tonight, I bring you some good news. I didn't hear it from the pollsters or the columnists. I read it this past week on the faces of countless people like you across this country.

The good news is that we are going to win this election. The good news is that in 1972 we will take the government out of the hands of the special interests and restore it to the people.

We will win because our side has the stirring voice of Ted Kennedy.

We will win because our side has the boundless heart of Hubert Humphrey.

We will win in Minneapolis because of the drive and determination of your remarkable young governor, Wendell Anderson.

We will win here because we are standing with that brilliant and decent man, Fritz Mondale, and with Congressmen and other candidates in the best tradition of the Democratic Party.

Most of all, we will win because we love America enough to call her to a higher standard.

We don't have John Connally with us. We don't have the oil barons and the big money. The Republicans have them—and they are welcome to them. If that crowd ever came out for me, I'd know I was on the wrong track.

I want the rubber workers and the steelworkers, the small businessmen, the senior citizens, the young people, and all those who live by honest toil instead of living off tax loopholes.

It was the people—not Wall Street—who elected Franklin Roosevelt in 1932.

It was the people—not Wall Street—who elected Harry Truman in 1948.

And it will be people—not Wall Street—who elect the Democratic national ticket in 1972.

So let us draw strength from the memory of others who have set out before us on the same journey.

Let us draw strength from the memory of the man who called us to "make gentle the life of the world"—my dear friend, Robert Kennedy.

Let us draw strength from the memory of that great and gallant man who showed us we could trust and love a president of the United States—John F. Kennedy.

And let us draw strength from the deep commitment of President Truman and President Johnson to the education of our children and the equality of our citizens.

This election is not going to be decided by ITT. This election is not going to be decided by the manipulators and the special interests. This election is not going to be decided by giant corporations like General Motors or by a corrupt dictator like General Thieu. This election is going to be decided by men and women who want their land to turn away from injustice to the blessings of decency and peace.

So I say here again tonight: Come home, America, from the

longest, the cruelest, and the stupidest war in our national history.

I make you this solemn pledge: Within ninety days of the inauguration, we will bring every American soldier and prisoner home from Indochina.

And I make another pledge to you: Once this conflict is over, never again will we commit the precious young blood of this land to bail out a corrupt dictatorship ten thousand miles away.

Then we can begin the redemption of our own great but deeply troubled land.

Since 1969, two million workers have been forced out of work. Six million Americans have been forced onto welfare.

And this is my answer: We will guarantee a job opportunity for every man and woman in America who is able to work.

In the last three and a half years, our people—especially the old living on fixed incomes, and growing young families—have felt the pain of wartime inflation. The Nixon inflation is ground into every pound of hamburger you buy.

I say that we must have an even-handed attack on inflation —one that controls prices and profits and interest rates, and not just the wages you earn.

Come home, America, from government for the privileged to government for the people.

The American revolution began with the rallying cry: No taxation without representation.

Today we renew that struggle, and we say: No taxation without justice.

There is something fundamentally wrong with a tax system that permits a corporate executive to deduct his twenty-dollar martini lunch while a working man cannot deduct the price of his bologna sandwich.

And there is something wrong with a property tax system that makes home ownership a pain rather than a joy.

I do not believe in the Nixon answer—a national sales tax that will cost the average family $200 a year.

Let us build instead a tax system that asks not one penny

more from rank-and-file taxpayers, but finally asks the big and the powerful to pay their fair share.

Come home, America, from the betrayal of public trust to the integrity of public service.

I am tired of government which proclaims one course in public while plotting a different course in secret.

We have had a secret plan for peace since 1969—but that plan will forever remain a secret to the 20,000 Americans and the countless Vietnamese killed since 1969. When we read about Mr. Nixon's gigantic bomber raids that are pounding the people of Indochina, let us remember that those people, too, are the children of God.

We have seen secret deals with ITT and the special interests —and they have rewarded our opposition with a $10 million secret campaign fund.

We do not know who contributed that money or how it will be spent. I assume that officers of ITT are on the list. If they aren't they are the most remarkable political ingrates in American history.

We do know that $114,000 of that secret Nixon fund went to the men who were arrested invading our national Democratic headquarters in the dark of night with their wiretapping equipment, their burglary tools, and their rubber gloves.

Our campaign is a people's campaign. We are not looking for a $10 million secret fund. The next administration is not for sale.

Instead, we are looking for a million ordinary Americans who will contribute $25—or whatever they can afford, even if it's 25 cents—not because they want special favors for themselves, but because they want a better land for us all.

With your support and your votes, I know we can bring America home. We can elect a president whose heart beats for all our people, not just for the privileged few.

What do the Republicans offer?

At their recent convention, they took up the cry "Four more years."

But think about American sons and Asian children dying in Vietnam.

Can we afford four more years of that?

Think about hungry children, and young G.I.'s hooked on heroin, and mothers who can't pay the grocery bill.

Can we afford four more years of that?

Think of the wiretappers, the warmongers, and the purveyors of racial fear.

Can we afford four more years of that?

Think of lonely old people living in poverty, of strong young people forced into idleness, of a welfare system that is unfair both to those it seeks to serve and to those who pay its cost.

Can we afford four more years of that?

The real question is what kind of country we want.

Three thousand years ago, the ancient prophet said it this way: "I have set before you life and death, blessing and cursing. Now choose life, so that you and your seed may live."

We occupy only a small part of a small planet almost lost amid a great stream of stars, but we have added something unique and special to the meaning of existence.

In this tiny corner of the universe, we have stood against eternal night and affirmed that life can be free—and life can have purpose.

Now let us strengthen our way of life, so that we may preserve it.

Let us bless our country, so that all our countrymen may secure the full blessings of liberty.

Let us glow with love for the best in America, so that we may bring a new spirit to the life of the world.

The journey will be long and difficult—but I believe that we can go home again.

In two centuries as a nation, we have fought the wars we had to fight.

We have tried to feed the hungry, to shelter the homeless, and to open an opportunity for every American to earn a decent standard of life.

We cannot give up now. Now, in 1972, we can make America work again.

I was a bomber pilot in World War Two. And I still remember the day when our plane was crippled so badly by antiaircraft fire that the crew was ready to bail out. I was scared, but I thought we could make it back.

So I gave this order to the crew: "Resume your stations, we're going to bring this plane home."

We have passed through hard and troubled years. But tonight, I say to you and to people everywhere who love this land: "Resume your stations. We're going to bring America home."

LOOKING AHEAD

Oxford Speech

I was invited to lecture at Oxford the day after President Nixon's second inauguration. The reaction to my speech there and in the English press generally was strongly favorable. The reaction at home was also strong, but much of it was negative. Perhaps the reason was not principally what I said, but that I said it abroad. Or perhaps people felt that with the election behind us, the issues of the election were beyond debate—at least by the losing candidate.

My purpose at Oxford was not to rewage the campaign, but to draw from my reflections some perspective on the future course of the country. In the midst of the criticism that followed, a colleague in the Senate told me not to worry—that the speech would "wear well with time." And by the early summer, in the wake of Watergate, my office was receiving constant requests for it. The warnings about "one-man rule," "the exhaustion of institutions," and the need to reassert legislative power no longer seemed either alarmist or bitter. They had become instead the central concerns of the nation.

Oxford University

OXFORD, ENGLAND | JANUARY 21, 1973

American Politics: A Personal View

I had hoped to be occupied elsewhere today. But the American electorate has made it possible for me to spend this time with you.

Had my fellows citizens been better acquainted with your history, they might have seen certain parallels between Richard Nixon and his namesakes who sat on the English throne.

Like Richard I, Richard Nixon has been celebrated for his foreign journeys, while his own land has been troubled and unattended.

Like Richard II, who wasted England's wealth in a failing war in Ireland, Richard Nixon has squandered America's good name in a foolish venture in Indochina.

And like Richard III, if we can believe the Tudor historians, Richard Nixon has usurped powers that are not his in law or tradition.

You have been spared a King Richard IV. We seem to have him—for four more years.

Just why the American electorate gave the present administration such an overwhelming mandate in November remains something of a mystery to me. I do not expect to find a fully satisfactory answer. We worked so incredibly hard, and campaigned so fairly and openly, that our overwhelming defeat has left us with a temporary sense of sadness and fury that we must learn to direct into a constructive, continuing effort to restore the best hopes of America. I firmly believed throughout 1971 that the major hurdle to winning the presidency was winning the Democratic nomination. I believed that any reasonable Democrat could defeat President Nixon. I now think that no one could have defeated him in 1972. And I am not certain that the Democratic Congress will hold him in check for the next four years. I am convinced that the United States is closer to one-man rule than at any time in our history—and this paradoxically by a president who is not popular.

Fundamentally, we have experienced an exhaustion of important institutions in America. Today only the presidency is activist and strong, while other traditional centers of power are timid and depleted. This is why one man in the White House was able for so long to continue a conflict of madness in Southeast Asia hated by so many of his countrymen.

The institution of Congress has been exhausted by executive encroachment and legislative paralysis. For a decade, a war was waged without Congressional approval; for years, that war raged on in part due to Congressional inaction. The representatives of the people proved unwilling to end a policy opposed by the people.

But the impotence of Congress and the omnipotence of the presidency have deeper roots and a longer history. In 1933, the Senate and the House passed Administration bills almost before they were printed or read. It was a time of crisis. But in the years since then, the Congress has acted as though the crisis were permanent. We now accept the curious notion that the legislative initiative rests with the executive branch. Indeed, students of American government are themselves surprised at the startling fact that nearly 90 percent of the legislation the Congress considers originates with the Administration.

And in the last generation, presidential activism and Congressional passivity have been even more pronounced in the field of foreign policy. Congress was not asked for approval in the 1950's before American troops were dispatched to Korea and Lebanon. The chairman of the Senate Foreign Relations Committee, who advised against the Bay of Pigs invasion, was ignored, while other members of Congress were not even consulted. The Senate was assured that the Gulf of Tonkin Resolution was no writ for a wider war; it was then used as an excuse for the widest war since 1945.

Now this tide—which has ebbed and flowed for four decades —has crested at a new high. Just before Christmas, the President, in the flush of his electoral landslide, unleashed the most barbarous bombing of the war without even forewarning the Congress. He then refused to explain it or to permit any of his subordinates to explain it—a situation which must strike you especially as strange, since not only the foreign secretary but the prime minister are regularly called to account in the House of Commons.

I only wish your government had expressed to us the moral outrage that a good friend was obligated to express against the Nixon destruction of Indochina. Thank God for the eloquent and timely words of Roy Jenkins.

The President's defense for silence over this arbitrary bombardment and secret negotiations was the American doctrine of executive privilege, which is supposed to protect certain limited types of communication within the executive branch. The truth is that he was abusing executive privilege, which is not supposed to prevent review and the exercise of responsibility by the legislative branch.

Our Constitution, like yours, is an organic document. Although the first Americans sketched the essential outlines of government, they wisely left the embellishment of the relationship among its three branches to experience. Thus, the assignment of specific authority is only in a few instances explicit.

But among the rights clearly assigned to the Congress are the powers of war and peace and the power of the purse. The power to make or unmake war, however, has been stripped almost completely from the Senate and the House. And now, for the first time, the executive has mounted a serious challenge to the Congressional control of appropriations. Perhaps the Congress invited this attack by a complacent acquiescence in the Vietnam disaster; in any case, the battle is on, and the Congress is losing.

Last fall, we submitted to the President a bill to clean up our nation's waterways. He vetoed the bill, and we passed it again over his veto. He then simply refused to spend the money as Congress directed. The success of this tactic was followed by the impoundment of funds for other domestic programs. Most incredibly, at the end of the last legislative session the President demanded that the Congress rubber-stamp such impoundments in advance. He asked us to agree to set a budgetary ceiling within which the sole power of appropriation was reserved to the executive branch. Even more incredible was the speed with which the House of Representatives approved this request, and its relatively narrow defeat in the Senate. And after Congress refused the President this authority, he just took it. One wonders why he even bothered to ask.

This is not the way of a government of laws or even of men, but of one man. Today the United States is moving dangerously in that direction. The Congress seems incapable of stopping what it opposes or securing what it seeks. It has been described by a Republican senator as a "third- or fourth-rate power" in Washington. And it may be fairly asked whether the Congress of the United States in the seventh decade of this century is in peril of going the way of the House of Lords in the first decade. The difference is that the diminution of the Lords made English government more democratic, while the diminution of the Congress makes American government more dictatorial.

And the exhaustion of the Congress is matched by the exhaustion of the political parties.

The Republican Party, reduced to utter vassalage by the White House, offers little more than administrative reorganization. They offer the politics of efficiency—but to what end and impact? Their answer to the transportation crisis is to rearrange the Department of Transportation. Their answer to desperate social needs is to reduce and rename social programs. Their answer to the threat of racism is the malignancy of benign neglect. Their answer to the housing crisis is a moratorium on new public housing.

And at the same time, the loyal opposition is neither loyal to a specific set of ideas nor effective in its opposition. The Democratic Party is in peril of becoming a party of incumbency out of power, much like the Whigs of the nineteenth century—a party with no principles, no programs, living only from day to day, caring only for the perquisites of office, doing nothing—and worse, not caring that nothing is done.

Though important and, I believe, enduring reforms have opened the Democratic Party to broader citizen participation, the purposes for which it stands remain disputed and undefined. For twenty-eight of the last forty years, those purposes were set by Democratic presidents in the White House. Today, the party consists largely of fragments and factions, often still divided along the same lines as in 1968, when pro-Administration and antiwar forces contended for its soul.

At the same time, Democratic constituency has declined; in both of the last national elections, the Democratic candidate could count only 40 per cent of the vote. I believe the party is still the best hope and help of the unprivileged majority of Americans. Yet I know that we have failed to convey the Democratic appeal to millions who are not racist, but afraid; who do not seek a Wallace, but will settle for him if no one else seems to hear or heed them.

And what is the response of the Democratic Party and its major ally in organized labor? Not a determined effort to shape a constituency for change, but an exhausted armistice with the status quo. In 1973, the party itself is no longer a challenging source of ideas and innovation in society. Indeed, in the midst of the quarrels and the contention, the safest course for party officials has been to emphasize that they are interested not in the ideology but in the technology of politics.

Without principles, there is no party. And a nation cannot be led nobly or even decently by a collection of politicians whose highest purpose is power.

But perhaps the most discouraging development of recent years is the exhaustion of the institution of the press.

Under constant pressure from an administration that appears to believe that the right of a free press is the right to print or say what they agree with, the media have yielded subtly but substantially. During the campaign, I was subjected to the close, critical reporting that is a tradition in American politics. It was not always comfortable, but it is always necessary. Yet Mr. Nixon escaped a similar scrutiny. The press never really laid a glove on him, and they seldom told the people that he was hiding or that his plans for the next four years were hidden. Six days after the Watergate gang was run to the ground, Mr. Nixon invited reporters into his office, and submitted to the only interrogation his managers allowed during the fall campaign. Not a single reporter could gather the courage to ask a question about the bugging and burglary of the Democratic National Committee. Much of this can be blamed on the incestuous character of the White House press corps itself. Ask one wrong question and a reporter may find himself cut off altogether, thus ending his repose in one of the cushiest assignments a journalist can draw.

Now, with the election over, the executive branch has tightened the pressure on the media. For example, the Administration has expressed an intention to punish offending television networks by depriving their stations of licenses. Already, the White House has dismantled the Public Broadcasting System whose public affairs presentations the President found irritating. And the press has responded by retreating. It has catalogued the slashes in domestic programs and the plans for arbitrary, insensitive government—but it has not even noticed anything amiss in the fact that these steps were concealed or denied before the election. There are, of course, brave reporters, newspapers, and television channels ready to take the heat. But there are countless others who have left the kitchen for a more comfortable, uncritical existence in the antechamber of this administration. They are trying to get along by going along. The more wrong-headed and irresponsible are far more interested in cultivating their dubious "sources" on the inside than they are in presenting accurate information or thoughtful judgments. Fortunately, their reading audience is small and increasingly wary of ill-informed gossip.

And the exhaustion of American institutions is matched by an exhaustion of the American spirit.

This even touches some liberal intellectuals, traditionally the most tireless group in America. Today you can hear such liberals saying that government cannot make any real difference for good in the lives of people—that whatever it touches will turn to failure. Many of those who supported the advances of the 1960's so fervently now denounce with equal fervor the setbacks of the 1960's. And they are reluctant to resume the imperfect but important march interrupted by the war. Instead they seem almost happy to fulfill the prophecy of W. R. Inge, the Gloomy Dean, that he who would marry the spirit of the age soon finds himself a widower. And they seem to draw a curious personal consolation from the evidence that my appeals to the idealism and morality of America were rejected by the majority of Americans.

Indeed, these so-called liberals now tell us that we should not try to save our cities, cure the causes of crime, eradicate poverty, or admit our error in Vietnam. They say that if we are part of the solution, then we are also part of the problem. Their motto appears to be: "Nothing ventured, nothing lost." They seem to be searching for the lowest common denominator of the current political mood.

The same dispirit envelops millions of other Americans. They have followed a bloody trail of disappointment from a sunny street in Dallas to a hotel kitchen in Los Angeles. Three times they have voted for peace; each time they have been given more war. They were oversold on the social experiments of the 1960's; now they are wary of buying even sensible and essential social progress from any political leader. They see government as at best an annoyance, at worst an enemy, and they wish it would just leave them alone. Broken promises have ended in broken power. Public officials are viewed principally as annoying tax collectors.

To my mind, this mood was central to the outcome of the 1972 election. For example, the commentators have suggested that credibility was among my principal difficulties during the campaign. I agree, but not with the proposition that people did not believe me. I think they *did* believe that I would do what I said, and they were afraid. Many Americans looked back at the debris of the last decade, and they feared that once again they were about to face a hard effort and harvest nothing from it.

So to me the central challenge for the future of American politics is to end the paralysis of institutions and ease the apprehensions of the electorate. The United States must find a way to replace exhaustion with energy, cynicism with hope, resignation with determination, destructive anger with constructive activism.

That is so easy to say, so hard to do.

I no longer think it can be done merely by calls to greatness or appeals to idealism, no matter how eloquent. Americans have been told until they are tired of hearing it that they shall overcome, that they can move their country forward, that they can have a great society, that they can seek a newer world or find the lift of a driving dream—or even bring America home to its founding ideals. This kind of summons has value; indeed, in my view, Americans are desperately anxious to believe in a transcendent, almost mystical purpose. But they are also skeptical now of any such summons unless there are signs of progress already there.

As I discovered in the last campaign, it is not even enough to outline proposals in specific detail. The only way to reawaken faith in the system is for government and politicians to restore it step by step, through substantive advances that mean something to people. They must see their sons home from Vietnam, their neighborhood crime rate reduced, their taxes used to build better lives instead of bigger bureaucracies, their children educated in decent schools, and their illnesses cared for at reasonable cost. The progress must be visible, sure, and steady. The words of politicians must be matched by effort.

This requires above all else a determined effort to improve

and strengthen the institutions in America that are supposed to serve the citizens of America. After a decade of disillusion, institutions may be unfashionable things. But institutions are not evil; they are neutral. And they are indispensable instruments of change in society. More often than not, the ebbs and tides of history are determined by the nuts and bolts of government.

In modern times, when American liberals have recognized that truth, they have tended to see it in terms of the presidency. Only a few years ago, liberal scholarship still celebrated the strong executive and sought to strengthen it even more. Now we have learned that the presidency, too, is a neutral instrument—that power in the White House can be abused as well as used, that a reactionary or a warmaker can also read Richard Neustadt and James McGregor Burns.

Twice now our answer has been an attempt to change the person in the presidency. Both times we have ended in at least as much difficulty as we were in before. It is now almost four years until the next national election. It is also time to ask whether American progressives should continue to rely on a quadrennial chance to capture what is becoming an elective dictatorship.

We may lose again as we have before. And liberty is the real loser when so much authority is vested in a single office.

There will be plenty of time to prepare for the next campaign. But now is the time for a determined effort to change not the person in the White House, but the power of the presidency. American liberals must reverse the forty-year trend toward a stronger president and return to the two-hundred-year-old tradition of shared power. It is time to renew the Constitution, the Bill of Rights, and the Declaration of Independence.

The Supreme Court is subject to fate and executive appointment, with only the Senate standing between the court and an ideological coup. So the true priority is to protect the place of the Congress in the federal system. We must seek a pluralism of power, where Congress and the president guard and prod each other. And there must be a new devotion to personal liberty and personal privacy in America.

Some political scientists claim that this is the wrong aim. They say: Only the president can lead because only the president has a mandate. But Congress has a collective mandate, made by a blend and balance of the regional interests reflected in each member's election. And that collective mandate can be as effective as the president's universal mandate. The Congress can work to check the executive and to move the country. It can seek cooperation with the president; it can also shape a kind of cooperative tension with him that can make change happen. In the words of an ancient philosopher: "That which is in opposition is in concert, and from things that differ comes . . . harmony."

In pursuit of a pluralism of power, the Congress has powerful weapons at its disposal. And after executive provocation without peer or precedent, the legislative branch at long last seems ready to act.

Now the Congress must exert its authority to achieve a full measure of influence. For example, when the legislation that allows the president to control wages and prices comes up for renewal, the Senate and the House should not issue another blank check. We should include safeguards to assure that profits, dividends, and interest rates are never again permitted a special break while the wages of workers bear the full burden.

But the Congress should not wait for such opportunities. It should mount a consistent and coherent effort, founded on its foremost power—control over appropriations. James Madison wrote in *The Federalist Papers,* number 58:

"The power over the purse may, in fact, be regarded as the most complete and effectual weapon with which any constitution can arm the immediate representatives of the people, for obtaining a redress of every grievance, and for carrying into effect every just and salutary measure."

This insight is borne out in the history of your own land. For five centuries, from Edward I to George III, English liberty was purchased piece by piece by the Parliamentary power of the purse. And in 1973, the Congressional power of the purse can sustain American liberty.

It can be used to stop the abuse of executive privilege. Part or perhaps all of an appropriation could be conditioned on the administration's consent for the appropriate officials to testify before House and Senate committees.

It can be used to stop executive wars by whim. The Congress must refuse to fund conflicts it has not declared or even decided to fight. From the tragedy and travail of Vietnam, the Congress at least must learn the truth of Edmund Burke's warning: "The thing you fight for is not the thing which you recover; but depreciated, sunk, wasted and consumed in the contest." American ideals have been depreciated. American wealth has been sunk. Human lives have been wasted, and Indochina itself has been consumed in the contest. The United States must fight when the course is right. But never again should the Congress allow young American lives to be lost for the defense of a corrupt dictator anywhere in the world.

And these steps are only a beginning. For if the Congress is to assume a role of leadership, it must have not only the negative power to review and reverse policy, but also the positive power to make policy in the first place. It must know enough— so it will not hear the reply that the president always knows best. It must be structured for integrated decision-making— so it will not hear the reply that only the president can pull all the pieces together.

First, the Congress should establish a unified budget assessment mechanism. The Senate and House should establish a committee to estimate revenues, set a general level of expenditures, and establish priorities to relate specific appropriation decisions to that general level. This committee should have sufficient resources of expertise and information. There is no reason to let the president control the budget because he has the only Office of Management and Budget.

Second, the Congress should establish a similar mechanism for national security policy. With members drawn from the Appropriations, Foreign Relations, and Armed Services Committees, such a unified committee could offer a thoughtful and sensible alternative to executive proposals. This committee, too, should have the necessary resources. If the president can have two state departments, the Congress can have at least one agency to provide information and recommendations about foreign affairs and defense policy.

Third, the Congress should adjust the seniority system. No other legislative body in the Western world uses length of service as the sole standard for place and power in its committees. If the Congress is to carry out its collective mandate it must do what the mandate means, not what a few individuals from safe districts want. An activist, effective Congress must reflect the popular will. It cannot do so unless the members freely elect committee chairmen.

Finally, the Congress should defend its powers as it extends them. It must consider and choose from a number of alternatives to cancel or control the impoundment of its appropriations. Only then can the Congress assure the execution of the policies it has enacted.

So if the Congress has the will, there is a way to exercise positive leadership. For the long term, the question is—in what direction?

I am convinced still that the society to which America should aspire is a liberal one. To those who charge that liberalism has been tried and found wanting, I answer that the failure is not in the idea but in the course of recent history. The New Deal was ended by World War Two. The New Frontier was closed by Berlin, Cuba, and an imaginary missile gap. And the Great Society lost its greatness in the jungles of Indochina.

Of course, liberal programs will sometimes fail anyway, for human decisions are frail always. Government is the creation of men and encompasses the weaknesses of men. Plans can be poorly executed—though a Congress with sense and a bit of intelligence can work to prevent that. But that government is best, I believe, that best serves the demands of justice. So what Americans should seek is a system in which the principles of civil equality and individual liberty have the highest claim on statesmanship. We must strive to provide a decent standard of life for all citizens and to redistribute wealth and power so each citizen has a fair share. And along with this must come a foreign policy which puts humanity and morality ahead of Cold War myths and the prestige of leaders who would rather compound error than face reality.

And not only can an institutional revival of the Congress lead America in a new direction; it can also spark a similar institutional revival outside government.

Where power is pluralistic rather than presidential, the press will not have so much to fear from the executive branch. It could institute reforms such as the rotation of correspondents at the White House and among candidates in a national election, and the assignment of political reporters and not just "regulars" to the president during a campaign.

There are also hopeful signs of a reawakening in the Democratic Party. The party is scheduled to hold biennial conferences to set national policy, with the first one next year.

And as Democrats look ahead to 1976, they can be encouraged by the enduring gains of 1972. For I believe my campaign set the manner in which future candidates must seek the Democratic nomination—openly, candidly, not with the traditional strategy of saying as little as possible but with a pledge to seek and speak the truth. I believe we also set a standard for the conduct of future campaigns—which will have to reveal their contributors and represent the people rather than the politicians. And, hopefully, Americans will not again accept wiretapping, Watergates, and the spectacle of a candidate hiding in the White House. Instead, they will expect at least a commitment to correct wrongs rather than committing them. Finally, I believe our campaign set forth the great issues that will dominate the debate of the 1970's, ranging from tax reform to a rational military budget.

And millions of Democrats, whether they are ordinary citizens or senators, are anxious to carry the banner. I have faith that their energy and efforts can end the exhaustion of the electorate, enlist the country in a coalition of conscience as well as self-interest, and expand the twenty-eight million votes the national ticket won in 1972 into a majority that is right as well as new.

In 1972, I was the beneficiary of the most devoted, idealistic campaign workers ever assembled. They provided the energy and the tough-minded attention to issues and political organization that enabled me to win the Democratic presidential nomination against all the odds-makers and political prophets. They did not prevail in November; they remain, however, closest to the enduring spirit of the nation that we ought to honor in the year of our bicentennial, 1976. They are the most effective, dynamic political force in American politics today. No one will win either the Democratic presidential nomination in 1976 or the subsequent presidential election as a Democrat without the active support of this superbly motivated, public-spirited force of Americans.

But as I have noted, the next election is four years away. For the immediate future, the key is the Congress. It must take the initiative and provide the inspiration. It must cure the paralysis and procrastination that have earned it the doubt, the disrespect, and the cynicism of the American people. *The New York Times* recently described the President as a leader who "behaves with the aloofness of a Roman emperor." It is useful to remember that no Roman emperor was crowned until the Roman senate abdicated.

Before most of you were born, the late Henry Luce described this time in history as the American century. Since then, the United States has learned the hard way that you cannot colonize centuries any more than you can colonize countries.

But I would still like to believe that my country has something of value to offer to a beleaguered world.

It is not just our wealth and our technology—though that we should share with those who need it.

And it is not the terrible gift of another Guernica in Indochina.

And surely it is not our power to unleash a nuclear reign of terror, to give the earth a last shimmering moment of light before the endless night.

Throughout our history, America's greatest offering—as I said in accepting the Democratic presidential nomination—has been as "a witness to the world for what is noble and just in human affairs." This is what summoned the dock workers of Manchester to support Abraham Lincoln and the cause of liberty during our Civil War. And this is what America must restore. If we fail, other generations who are not free will look back and say that things cannot be any other way.

So, in my mind, the challenge of the American future is to revive our institutions and resume our progress at home while we act abroad with "a decent respect for the opinions of mankind."